Cover Photograph

Wet snowflakes over the dark background of **Robber's Roost** tell the story of those who followed the 1883 gold mining boom to the upper New River watershed. Nellie Ladd titled the photograph **"Coming Down."**

Robber's Roost is the stuff of legend. It was at this point on the western trail to the upper New River mines that in 1889 one of the ex-laborers of the Ladds' Mountain Boomer Mine held up the mail carrier, David Gray. Robber Eric Erikson had quit his job two weeks before, after hearing that Frank Ladd was going to send out a shipment of $10,000 in gold from the Boomer. But Erikson's efforts only got him minimal loot, because Frank had become suspicious of foul play and sent the gold east instead, over the divide with the pack train to Callahan. Another man accused of the mail heist was exonerated, and Erikson was captured, but he escaped from jail in San Francisco, never to be found again.[1]

In about 1913, Robber's Roost expanded to become the last community built to house miners in the area. It was the home base for the Tener Mine, principally a placer mining operation whose two metal pipe monitors pounded the gravel of Slide Creek to sluice for gold. The Tener brothers also had a hardrock gold mine.

The spot is now a level forested area with small depressions where cellars used to hold stores for the winter. Since the latest fire to pass through the area, in 1999, the Trinity Alps Wilderness is taking back the forest. Retired U.S. Forest Service archeological technician Gay Holland Berrien has not only guided colleagues and friends in meticulous site studies and mapping of the now empty town and mine sites in the wilderness, but has catalogued and exhibited Nellie Ladd's photographs, most of them now housed with the Trinity County Historical Society in Weaverville, California. The cultural history in site studies, photographs, century-old articles from local newspapers, and tales and transcripts of stories by old-timers hold many of the secrets hidden in woods, meadows, and canyons where almost no structures remain, victims of moisture, erosion, mud and snow slides, scavenging and forest fires.

Nellie Ladd's photographs of Robber's Roost are representative of her prolific late period of photography (1913-1920), reflecting progressive sophistication of technique and a growing sense of photography as historical record. See other photographs on pages 55 and 153 (Robber's Roost) and 80, 81, 83, 85 (Tener Mine).

---

1. Gay Holland, "The Tenner Camp," *Klamity Kourier*, July 7, 1971; Gay Holland Berrien e-mail, May 27, 2002.

(Nellie Ladd photograph) Grover,
Willard Ladd guide the mule train
across Mary Blaine Meadow.
Pony Buttes backdrop. c. 1907.

Nellie E. Ladd

MINING CAMP PHOTOGRAPHER OF THE TRINITY ALPS   1859 -1922

Text, Design, Photographs:
Valerie Budig-Markin

19th-20th Century Photographs:
Ellen "Nellie" Elizabeth Ladd

Naturegraph Publishers, Inc.
Happy Camp, CA

Cover photograph by Nellie Ladd: "Robber's Roost in the snow, self-titled, 'Coming Down'" (c. 1915).
Cover Signature "Nellie E. Ladd": Ellen "Nellie" Elizabeth Ladd wrote her signature in a *Third Reader*, California State Series of School Textbooks, published by the State Board of Education of the State of California in 1886. She probably taught her sons from this text during their home schooling when there was no public teacher in Old Denny. The signature "Nellie E. Ladd" was transposed from the textbook (a gift from Smokey Bergstrom to the author) to the cover of the present book and included in its title.

Nellie E. Ladd: Mining Camp Photographer of the Trinity Alps   1859 -1922
Copyright © 2004 by Valerie Budig-Markin

Budig-Markin, Valerie.
  Nellie E. Ladd : mining camp photographer of the Trinity Alps, 1859-1922 / text, design, photographs by Valerie Budig-Markin ; 19th-20th century photographs, Ellen "Nellie" Elizabeth Ladd.
      p. cm.
  Includes bibliographical references and index.
  ISBN 0-87961-269-X -- ISBN 0-87961-266-5 (pbk.)
  1. Ladd, Nellie E. (Ellen Elizabeth), 1859-1922. 2. Photographers--United States--Biography. 3. Women photographers--United States--Biography. 4. Trinity Alps Region (Calif.)--Pictorial works. 5. Mining camps--California--Trinity Alps Region--Pictorial works. 1. Title

  TR140.L25B83 2004
  770'.92--dc22
  [B]

Photographs: Glass plates, negatives and original photographs by Nellie Ladd reprinted by permission from the Trinity County Historical Society. See "Photographs and Illustrations," pp. 167-168.
Copyrighted photographs by the author include: Figs. 6-2, 6-3, photos p. 144, Figs. 6-15, 6-16, 6-24, 6-26, 6-28, 6-30, 6-33, 6-36, 6-37, 6-38, 6-49, 6-53, 6-59, 6-60, 6-63, 6-65, 6-66. Photographs by Rob Robinson, pp. 155, 163 may only be used by written permission.
Copyrighted illustrations by the author include area sketch, p. 3; salamander, dogbane, p. 4; area sketch, p. 13; tin pitcher, china logo, bottle, p. 16; glass plate camera, family camera, p. 38; iron candleholder, p. 64. See "Photographs and Illustrations," pp. 167-68.
Photograph captions: names in parentheses are those of the respective photographers. Numbering of photographs hereafter refers to chapter and photographs in each chapter.

Published by: Naturegraph Publishers, Inc., Happy Camp, CA, U.S.A.

MINING CAMP PHOTOGRAPHER OF THE TRINITY ALPS   1859 -1922

Table of Contents

Acknowledgements

This project is the inspiration of Gay Holland Berrien, retired archeological technician of the U. S. Forest Service, Big Bar Ranger Station, who put all her research, knowledge and wisdom at my disposal, including her research on New River voters from the old Trinity County Great Registers (Appendix A). She guided me to a growing network of people interested in protecting the area and the treasure of history fading away in the upper reaches of New River, in the Trinity Alps Wilderness of northern California. With her help, I met Lowrie Gifford, Frank Wallen, and Ray "Smokey" Bergstrom, who, like Gay, her brother Ed and their father Dick Holland, knew the Ladd family and had personal effects and memories of the past. Gay introduced me to Greg Rumney of Chromogenics Photography, who gave me the best prints possible for the book from Nellie Ladd negatives, glass slides, and fading photographs, sometimes so dirty he had to remove small rocks from them. Jack Bentley, curator of the First Street Gallery of Humboldt State University, helped me through the maze of publishing options and advised me on layout, design, and issues of art, history, and financing. Gay's introduction to Willow Creek historians Margaret Wooden and Max Rowley helped us all solve historical puzzles, bringing different local histories into a common focus.

Gay Berrien's research expeditions to Old Denny in the summers of 1999 to 2003 were hosted the first year by the U. S. Forest Service and the rest mostly by Gay and her brother Ed Holland. Crew members included Pat and Ron Craig, Elaine and Bill Sundahl, John Palmquist, Sheryl O'Brien, Dana Supernowicz, Tim Laird, Trudy Vaughan, Barbara Woodrum, Susanne Rinne, Wayne Moss, James Barnes, Grant Davis, Howard May, Jeff Buchin, Suzanna Urminska, Alex Collins, Stephanie Low, Rob Robinson, Barbara Bergstrom and Randy Steinbeck. Jim Pellegrini was our principal pack train guide. On our 2002 expedition, Grant Davis, great-great-grandson of early miner Stephen Sherwood, helped record the Sherwood Mine site and shared family photographs for this book.

Peter Palmquist, founder and curator of the Women in Photography International Archive, first put about forty Nellie Ladd photographs into print and advised Gay Berrien on her traveling Nellie Ladd photo exhibit. This seed project's funding was furthered by the encouragement of summer research team regular, Peter's brother John Palmquist. The exhibit opened to over 2,500 visitors in seven different cities and five counties in northern California, and in Reno, Nevada. The spring of 2003 brought new friends into the picture in Barbara Bergstrom and Darlene and Leon Cody, who told stories of life at the Tough Nut Mine. In the summer of 2003 Rich Lorenz offered invaluable insight into the character and relationships of Nellie Ladd in a packet of 105 postcards from her personal effects. The Eureka *Times-Standard* publicized my Humboldt State University library exhibit of the cultural history surrounding Nellie Ladd photographs and brought Eureka relative of the Ladds, Michael Moore, his wife Catherine, and his father Robert Moore into the scope of this story.

The Trinity County Historical Society gave the Old Denny historical research a home and shared the Ladd photographs with me for this book. Yvonne Lillehaug, Susanne Rinne, Howard May and Gay Berrien read drafts of this first book and offered thoughtful advice. Humboldt State University gave me the semester sabbatical to begin the project, locate and restore photographs. Riley Quarles and the staff of the HSU Courseware Development Center gave me invaluable long-term technological assistance. While I researched and wrote this manuscript and collected the best prints of Nellie Ladd's photographs, my husband Bob Markin kept the home fires burning.

I offer the completed project with sincere thanks to you all.

(Photo V. Budig-Markin) Gay Berrien heads into the wilderness with her research team, summer, 2002.

This book is dedicated to
Gay Holland Berrien,
a light in the forest.

(Photo Ed Holland) Gay explains the layout of old mining camp sites to the author, summer, 2001.

Photo courtesy of Ed Holland.

Introduction

The following photographical history preserves over a hundred Nellie Ladd photographs taken on glass slides and negatives between about 1895 and 1920, mostly in and around the upper New River mining camps of Old Denny (New River City), Marysville and White Rock (Cœur) in northern California. As private collections of these photographs are relegated to dusty attics and the slides, negatives and photographs deteriorate, and many people are looking for ways to protect them from extinction. The Trinity County Historical Society, which also maintains a traveling exhibit of Nellie Ladd photographs and sponsors continuing research on the mining camps, has agreed to share these photographs with the public through the publication of this manuscript.

The book's historical text, accompanying Nellie Ladd's photographs, situates both photographs and photographer for a modern reader who may or may not know the upper New River area. It begins with the native Americans who lived in or traveled through the mining district, tells of the 1883 mining boom, Frank Ladd's leading role and marriage to Ellen "Nellie" Elizabeth Casey Graham in 1886. In **Chapters I and II** we also follow the photographer's life, children, photography and friends. **Chapter III** tells the story and presents photographs of the New River mines, both in their heyday and in their demise. **Chapter IV** gives voice to local characters and their stories, based on photographs, Grover Ladd interviews from the 1960s and local newspaper articles. **Chapter V** brings together many Nellie Ladd photographs of panoramas and bridges and offers its own bridge to the present. **Chapter VI, "New River Today,"** brings the Nellie Ladd history up to date through recent interviews, photographs and a text glimpsing the encounter of the present and the past. While so many of the physical artifacts and structures pictured in Nellie's photography are now lost, along with some of the storytellers, many others are stillpresent in (new) Denny, Old Denny and beyond, and sometimes one steps into the past just by rounding a bend of the trail and running into a pack train of mules. The story of the New River mining camps emerges as a treasure of the imagination, preserved for us today in its essence in the amateur photographs and postcards of a mining camp wife, mother, postal clerk, storekeeper, mine owner, elections clerk, home schooling teacher, loving and beloved friend.

Appendix A, listing **New River Voters 1872-1896,** was prepared by Gay Berrien from the Trinity County Great Registers in Weaverville, CA. Unfortunately, women could not yet vote, so they do not appear on the lists. Appendix B, the **1900 U. S. census** for the New River Precinct gives a better idea of families, boarders and occupations.

The research begun here will continue in a children's version of the present manuscript, a new text composed by local children who select their favorite Nellie Ladd photographs, just as I have, and write their own local history.

CHAPTER I

Making a Home in the Mountains of California

I**n** her photography dating from about 1895 to 1920, Ellen "Nellie" Elizabeth Casey Graham Ladd tells many stories of Old Denny and the upper New River mining district of the northern California mountain wilderness. In the region now officially designated as the Trinity Alps Wilderness Area, the gradual destruction of virtually all the structures of the hardrock gold mining days makes Nellie Ladd's century-old photographs invaluable records of cultural, as well as photographic, history. They hold the secrets of ambition, family and community life, survival stories, mining and building techniques and daily routine in a very uncommon world and in a magnificent setting. The changing perspective and use of the camera, evolving from glass plates to negatives, tell the history of amateur photography in the early stages of its development and distribution in isolated rural California.

The stories these photographs tell us today do so thanks to an extraordinary woman born February 10, 1859 in Portsmouth, New Hampshire in a Catholic household of laborers. It is likely that she and her parents, John and Ellen Casey, moved to the Boston area when she was very young. She grew up knowing early in life about religion (she kept a picture of the Pope), hard physical work, and the importance of family. She lived in a society fiercely proud of American independence, yet that looked to the cultural centers of New England and beyond, to Great Britain and continental Europe. Massachusetts, or "the great mountain" in Algonquin, offered the diverse cultural traditions of living native American Wampanoag and Nauset peoples and the nearly extinct Massachusets, all speaking Algonquin dialects. She would have heard of the Revolutionary War and was a child in the Civil War. She may have heard of the new state of Nebraska in 1867, and probably passed through Colorado before it became the "centennial" state in 1876. California, a state since 1850, continued to broadcast news of gold that reverberated over the decades and the mountain ranges to the East coast.

Responding to the call of the West, Nellie Casey had by the age of 15 experienced the adventure of crossing the country from the Atlantic Ocean to the Pacific.[1] She probably had a previous husband before her marriage to Frank Ladd, since she bore the name "Graham" when she married Frank in 1886 in San Francisco and, according to the 1900 census, had a child who died. In 1885, Frank was in San Francisco, so the couple may have met in the big city or, instead, may have met in the northern coastal Humboldt County, where Frank worked in logging and in commercial fishing (at the mouth of the Eel River), and they may have gone to San Francisco to get married and honeymoon in 1886. Frank was already well known throughout northern California for his famous hardrock gold mine, the Mountain Boomer, in the Trinity Alps. In January, 1885 the San Francisco *Evening Post* had taken up the story of Ladd and his friends from local newspapers,[2] spreading reports of a new California gold rush, triggered by news of Stephen Sherwood's 1882 discovery:

> "He [Stephen Sherwood] made some locations, communicated his find to his friends, prospectors came in, and with them Messrs. Clement, Clifford and Ladd. They discovered or purchased the Mountain Boomer, built an arastra [arrastra] and in a short time ground out $11,000, with a profit over all expenses of $8,000."

--San Francisco *Evening Post,* Jan. 2, 1885

It was the promise of the unknown that Nellie Ladd embraced in 1886 as she married fellow Catholic and New Englander, Frank Ladd, an "energetic and go-ahead fellow"[3] from Maine. Frank was also a versatile adventurer when he became a partner in his first mine, the Mountain Boomer. According to different accounts, he discovered and claimed the mine in 1882 and/or was invited to invest in it in the form of a rock-crushing arrastra to separate the gold from the white quartz ore.[4] He helped establish the town of New River City in May of 1883.[5]

In the summer or as late as October of 1886, the newlyweds left San Francisco, when the rivers were low before the winter precipitation. They headed north some 200 miles toward the mountainous wilderness, either by way of Redding and Weaverville, which were east of the Trinity Alps, or from the coast inland from Humboldt Bay or Trinidad. There were controversy and competition regarding the two approaches. Travelers could take the C. & O. Railroad train from San Francisco to Redding in ten hours for $9.00. Then they could take the stagecoach another 12 hours over 60 miles from Redding through Weaverville to North Fork ($10.00). The last 30-some miles took another ten hours by saddle ($3.00).[6] This trail went a few miles past North Fork to East Fork, north to Rattlesnake and then Grizzly, and finally up over the divide to New River, the entire last 30 miles being "one unbroken field of quartz."[7] It is possible that the Ladds came to New River this way, since it was shorter, and the Weaverville newspaper mentioned Frank Ladd and his news periodically. Mine claims were recorded there as well.

On the other hand, there was a "new trail" built in 1885 from the west, up New River, including bridges over both Virgin and Eagle creeks along the last twenty or so miles of the trail from the west.[8] The San Francisco *Mining and Scientific Press* of Dec. 6, 1884 describes the Eureka route favorably (and inaccurately, according to the *Trinity Journal*). The voyage by steamer from San Francisco to Eureka with a cabin cost $10.00 (steerage only, for $6.00). The ferry from Eureka to Arcata, across Humboldt Bay, cost the traveler 50 cents. Then the "80" miles to New River by saddle would cost another $10.00. But the *Trinity Journal* corrected the 80 miles inland to 110 and the cost for the four-day trail ride to be at least $20.00.[9] Frank Ladd's son tells of his father working in logging and fishing in Humboldt County and traveling up New River in 1883, so he did travel that way as well.[10] It seems most likely that the Ladds combined the two approaches, coming in from Redding all the way to Hawkins Bar and then up the New River along the new trail.

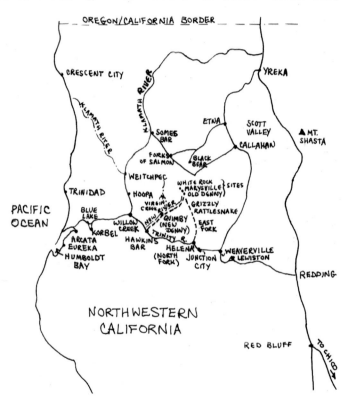

Fig. 1-1. (V. Budig-Markin) Area sketch: New River mines and northwestern California.

3

This anonymous photograph is believed to picture Nellie Ladd on horseback traveling the New River trail. Crossing treacherous rock slides, the trail rose through pine, cedar, fir and madrone forests, offering respite in the shadows where "Indian rhubarb" and tiger lilies now grow--and probably grew then--beside crystalline creeks. Streams offered the traveler a refreshing drink and an occasional glimpse of a curious trout minnow or a Pacific giant salamander. But one pressed on, for the creeks harbored mosquitos, too. Then the trails rose once again to  become dusty, rock-strewn paths overlooking wide panoramas of mountains and forests, bear grass, snowberries, crimson paintbrush and tiny pink dogbane.[11]

Fig. 1-2. (Anon.) Nellie Ladd
**traveling the treacherous trails
to the New River mines. c. 1900.**

 Whether Nellie Ladd first came to the New River mines by train or by ship, at least the last 30 miles of her trip, either from the east or the west, followed these hot, steep, narrow trails passable only by mule, by horse, or by foot. Snakes, deer, black bears, bobcats, coyotes, and foxes could meet one on a trail, and mountain lions may have watched the approaching couple from boulders or tree branches above. At the scent of a mountain lion, a horse might bolt, throw the rider, or lose its footing and fall, killing itself and its rider as well. Such could have been the fate of Frank Irving, a young friend of the Ladds who in 1910, at the age of 16, lost his life when his horse fell off the trail and probably crushed the boy beneath him.[12]

4

The Trinity mountains were a great cultural mix of peoples in continual flux. The native American people whose home was the upper New River and over the ridge into the Salmon River watershed were the New River Shasta. They were a Shasta-speaking people of Hokan stock.[13] The Chimariko, who may have been the first to enter the New River area, spoke the Hokan language and lived along the lower New River and the Trinity.[14] Sally Dyer, who married famed 1850s (and 1880s) miner Steve Noble, was at least half Chimariko; many Noble descendants mined, worked and studied in the New River district[15] *(see pages 108-110)*. Two Chimariko sisters from Cedar Flat on the Trinity River married white miners R. L. Thomas and Cyrus Quimby and moved into the mining camps.[16] The Hupa, of the Hoopa area, and the Southern Hupa, now calling themselves Tsnungwe, sometimes came into the New River watershed from the west, but most sources do not think their ancestral ground was there. They too married into the Chimariko.[17]

Fig. 1-3. (J. P. Harrington) Sally Noble.[18] 1921.

Fig. 1-4. (Nellie Ladd) Jim Chesbro at the Denny Store. c. 1915.

Nellie photographed Jim Chesbro, a trail clearer and later mail carrier, who was said to be a Hupa, as was A. Brizard's head mule train packer Bob Pratt.[19] The Hupa from the west, the Wintu from the southeast, the Karuk from the north and northwest had hemmed in the small New River Shasta and the Chimariko, peacefully assimilating them. By the time Nellie Ladd arrived only a few were still alive.[20] Miners had killed local Native Americans whose lifestyles were so different from their own and who opposed the destruction of salmon habitat by mining activities before the 1880s gold rush, and the U. S. Army probably killed New River Shasta on the Salmon River watershed during the Rogue River Indian Wars of 1850-1857.[21] Native inhabitants, perhaps from the north, had got the upper hand in Lake City, eight miles from New River City on Pony Creek, and drove out its white inhabitants in 1864.[22]

There was a Chinese camp near the New River mines where a hungry traveler might well stop to eat, as was the case in 1882 when Messrs. Kist and Kimball of Scott Valley were caught in snow at the top of the divide and forced to camp. They told the *Trinity Journal* that "the best meal they ever had in their lives was the dinner they took at the first camp they came to the next day," which was the Chinese camp.[23]

There were few Chinese hardrock mine owners but many worked in the mines. Grover Ladd remembered those who lived in White Rock, probably during his childhood in the early 1890s:

> "White Rock was just a camp, there was no mill there. Quite a few people lived there too--Chinese. They worked for the Uncle Sam and the Sherwood [Mines]. The Sherwood was the main mine. A lot of people worked on it."[24]

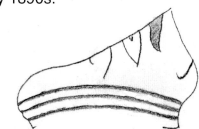

Fig. 1-5. (Gay Berrien) Sketch of Chinese tableware fragment at White Rock, Aug., 2001.

In 1885 Chinese placer miners were bringing in nearly 47% of the gold dust brought in to the store at Francis, about ten miles down New River from Denny.[25] Down on the Trinity River there were many Chinese placer miners. Today there is a "Joss House"[26]--"House of God"--state historical monument and museum in Weaverville dedicated to the Chinese community. Most Chinese county residents lived in Weaverville, Lewiston and Junction City. The 1890 census of North Fork (of the Trinity River) and the New River mining area, reported "89 Chinese, 453 Whites...62 Indians, 5 colored."[27] The 2001 archeological expedition to the White Rock area, where the store owner Alex Cœur (quoted above) conducted his business, located a single Chinese tableware fragment: a piece of an off-white rice bowl with light gray-blue lines and a partial pattern, which team members speculated could be that of bamboo, blue flowers, or circles and a dragonfly.[28] Another rice bowl fragment was found at the Ridgeway Mine, but its light green color and bamboo pattern were most likely a more modern imitation of a Chinese bowl.[29]

People of other cultural backgrounds were common. O. A. Swanson, Hans Block and John Miller were Swedish, John Hanson and Olaf Oman were Danish, and Charles Hanson was Norwegian. John Van Male was Dutch. Joseph Braw and John Vetore were Portuguese miners in the New River district and Frank Martin was from the Azores Islands. Alex Cœur, W. H. Levasseur and Joseph Francis were French, as were Peter Larcine's parents. Nellie Ladd's mother was French or French-Canadian, Archibald Fulmore was from Nova Scotia, and George Irving was from New Brunswick. Kate Irving, the Healys, the Hennesseys and Thomas Markham were Irish, and George Mowers and James Newton were Scottish. Captain Jim Franzen, Old Denny saloon keeper, and Al Lundberg were Prussian;[30] Charles Geyer and John Sharber were German. James Bonetti was Swiss. Gustave Gutzen was Russian.

A modern Trinity Alps Wilderness map shows the "new trail" built by Smith Brooks up New River. The trailhead (lower left) is about eight miles upstream from (New) Denny. The 11-mile trail crosses Virgin Creek (where the Chinese mined in the 1850s) at about three miles, Eagle Creek (nursery area for Pacific giant salamanders up to two feet long) at six miles, and then Robber's Roost, site of the cover photograph by Nellie Ladd. The trail continues past the mouth of Emigrant Creek at about eight miles, just after the site of the Emmons cabin (built after Nellie's death). Three more arduous miles of trail lead up to Old Denny.

During the 1880s wagon roads were built to connect Old Denny to various mines and to the town of Marysville and White Rock, two miles away. John Hennessey oversaw construction of a road connecting the Sherwood and Hunter mines to the Ridgeway stamp mill. Wagons were fabricated on site from wheels and axles transported up the trails by mules, since the approaches to the mines were all by narrow trail passable only by animal traffic.

The map shows mine sites that are all caved in today. One mine, the Gun Barrel, is located in error. Operated by the Ladds and Frank Patten, it was located over the Salmon divide (see the bold line at Mary Blaine Mtn.) several miles away. Willard and Grover wrote postcards home from Black Bear *(see area sketch, page 3)* and received them from their mother in Old Denny while working at the mine. *(See postcard, page 26.)*

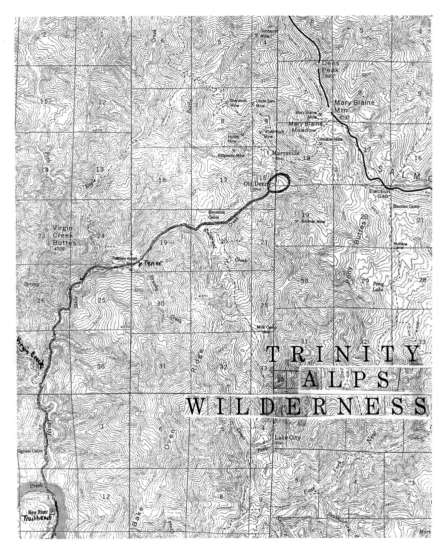

Fig. 1-6. New River trail today. From U. S. Forest Service wilderness map.

7

By 1886, when Nellie Ladd arrived, New River City was considered the most likely of the three little towns to "take the cake."[31] Business, as well as mining, was booming in the New River mining district, with a new two-story hotel in White Rock, owned by John McCulloch/McCullough. When Nellie first saw New River City, there was a store and hotel owned by Thomson and Cohen, a store and restaurant owned by Grant and Fringen, another store run by F.H. Loring, saloons owned by Boynton, Herrick, and Captain Franz(en), a restaurant owned by Dennis and Jackson, 20 miners' cabins, a sawmill, S. T. Hinkley's log chute, and a couple of other buildings.[32] At the height of the first building boom, construction was halted for a period of time due to a lack of nails.

Fig. 1-7. (Nellie Ladd) A snowy day in New River City (Denny). c. 1900. Glass plate. Furthest back on the left is Captain Jim Franz' saloon, then the Denny Store, the Ladd's house and perhaps Mullane's house, all four along the main street. Herrick's Saloon, which became the school, is on the right. In the far background, right, across the gulch from "downtown" Denny, is the Eureka Hotel.

The store for which New River City would be renamed was the Denny-Bar Mercantile Company or the "Denny Store," after one of its co-owners, A. H. Denny, a non-resident partner (with Abe Barr) in a chain of stores in New River City, Callahan, Cecilville, Fort Jones, Montague, Gazelle and Etna.[33]

Fig. 1-8. (Nellie Ladd) The Denny Store. Left to right: **Alex Boyd, Frank Ladd, Al Lundberg, Eugene Brackett, Earnest Piersol, Bert Brackett**. **c. 1900.** Glass plate.

Growth of the community was substantial in the early years. According to Nellie's son Grover more than a half century later, his father encountered as many as 300 people on one trip in to the mines during the "boom" in 1883. By 1886 the New River district had become a "permanent camp,"[34] with residents spending the winter, as well as the other seasons, living in the district. Conservative estimates of the population, based on the gold dust brought in by miners or on election counts, were around 500 in the three-town area, with other counts reaching as high as 10,000. Such estimates were like fish stories; each time the story was told, the numbers grew. One can also imagine the fluidity of the population, with people "coming all the time and building their little cabins" (*Trinity Journal,* 1/10/1885) in the woods and then moving on with the news of better finds, with the exhaustion of supplies, or having met with sudden, violent deaths.

Fig 1-9. (Nellie Ladd) Building in the wilderness. c. 1900.

Nellie and Frank settled first in a cabin a mile or less from New River City in the opposite direction from Marysville and White Rock, south across Slide Creek, the headwaters of New River, at the Mountain Boomer Mine. Their home was located on a slope above the confluence of two clear rocky streams, and its view of the valleys and mountains to the west must have been spectacular. A survey map dating from about the 1880s indicates the mines, the stamp mill and even the Ladd home, which does not exist today, having perhaps slid away with the erosion of the steep slope on which it stood. Remains of the Boomer sawmill and stamp mill lie near the few plate glass fragments of what may have been the Ladd home, which was located in approximately the lower left corner of this photograph. The cookhouse, above, with its tall sloping roof, was not built until 12 years after the Ladds moved to the Old Denny area. Even their first cabin may have been replaced by a mining operation building, since there are few flat sites for buildings, and the threat of deadly avalanches like the one in 1890 made the slope inhospitable for family life. Slopes were probably more covered with trees when the mining began in 1883. Perhaps already in 1886, when Nellie Ladd arrived, and certainly by 1902 they were deforested, their timber used for warmth, cooking and mining flumes, arrastras and buildings.

Fig 1-10. (Nellie Ladd) The Mountain Boomer Mine. Above: **cookhouse;** lower right: **stamp mill;** lower left or out of picture: **Ladd home site. c. 1902.** Glass plate.

The first two years of Nellie's life in the Trinity Alps brought gold, a family, new friends, and disaster. Almost as soon as she arrived at the mines, Nellie became pregnant. Her husband was named elections inspector in Forks of New River that fall of 1886.[35] The next summer, in June, Frank and Oliver Clemens made a surprising new gold strike when a corner of a ledge of gold-filled quartz was revealed as they dug a road to haul ore from the Tough Nut Mine to the Hard Tack.[36] The couple were in good spirits, then, when their first son, Grover Hayden, was born on July 1, 1887, both Nellie and her baby boy doing well despite the fact that there was no available doctor in the area. Grover may have been the first white child to be born in the New River mining district. Little Mary Larcine was almost a year old when her parents Peter and Celina moved to the area in 1884.[37] The Larcine Hotel was the center of the small town of Marysville.

By April, 1888, the miners of the New River district decided to tax residents to hire a physician who could practice both in their area and outside it. He was soon hired,[38] and Nellie was probably quite relieved, since she was already pregnant with her second child. Hopefully he was available to assist Nellie when Willard William was born, on January 17, 1889. On the other hand, the family lived far from town, and their home was probably deep in snow, the Mountain Boomer Mine being at a higher elevation than New River City.

"The first two years of Nellie's life in the Trinity Alps brought gold, a family, new friends, and disaster."

It was in the fall of 1889 that an important friendship would begin for Nellie when Kate Irving arrived with her husband George and three very young boys, George, Jr., James and Jarratt. George Irving and Frank Ladd would mine the Hidden Treasure together.[39]

Beginning in December, 1889, and continuing nearly every day until March, snow fell as much as seven feet at a time and nineteen feet in all. It was a dry snow, creating severe avalanche conditions.[40] On January 10, 1890, a day before Frank's 48th birthday and a week before Willard's first, a huge avalanche hit. John Lewis, who ran the boarding house at the Boomer Mine, was caught by the snow as he approached his home and, his wife watching in horror, was carried away; he was not found until the next day, having died deep in the snow, lodged against a tree. The Ladd cabin was hit and buried, and Frank, too, disappeared. Miraculously he survived. Someone remembered him saying he was going to clear snow away from one of the windows of the house, and everyone rushed out, digging frantically for four hours until they found him, unconscious, crushed against the house. He had breathed just enough air through the cracks in the walls to live but only regained consciousness after an entire night of efforts to revive him.[41] The Ladd family moved the very next day to New River City and then settled nearby at Butterfly Flat.[42] *(See sketch of the area, next page.)*

As soon as the family got situated at Butterfly Flat, Frank started working his mines again and soon after left for business in Chico. The *Trinity Journal* reported that Ladd would have to walk 100 miles to return home, "and the last 15 or 20 miles on snow shoes,"[43] by which they meant on skis. In the meantime, according to Grover, Nellie had company and help with her children from a young girl who was staying with the family. Still, in the snowy winter Nellie and her children must have depended somewhat on neighbors as they awaited Frank's safe return.

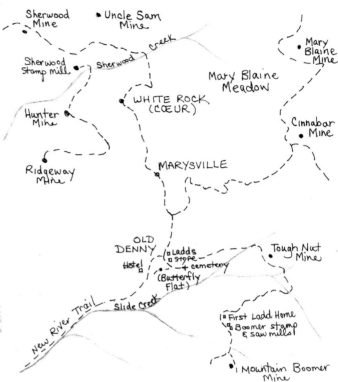

**Fig, 1-11. (V. Budig-Markin)
Sketch of the Old Denny area.**

Fig. 1-12. (Nellie Ladd) Left to right: **Frank, Grover and Willard Ladd on "snow shoes" or home-made skis. c. 1910.**

13

New River was a booming area. If there were, as an Irishman reported, four too few brothels and no church,[44] there were occasional Saturday night dances, square dances complete with calls of "all-a-man-left," pretty girls and love affairs.[45] Nellie took the boys to Mary Larcine's eighth birthday party in August, 1891. Also in attendance, according to "Aunty" in the *Trinity Journal* account of the event, were the Irving boys Jarratt and James, "Miss Nina Leas" (whose father worked for Frank at the Mountain Boomer), "Mrs. D M. Stoody, Mrs. John Anderson, Major Toms, George Dean, C. C.Dennis, John McCush, George Windham, Judge Yocum, William Mills and T. B. Markham." "Aunty" concluded, "All had a good, social time, and a better dinner I have not sat down to for some time. The hostess, Mrs. Larcine, knows just how to fix things up, and don't you forget it."[46] The New River public school was first opened in 1891 by G. C. Sarvis; it would move to other buildings later. The community attended a benefit dance and chicken dinner for the occasion in October.

Nellie took this school photograph in 1904, when Floy Lloyd was the schoolteacher.

Fig. 1-13. (Nellie Ladd) The Denny schoolhouse. c. 1904. Glass plate. Herrick's Saloon became the schoolhouse in 1904. (Left to right) **Hazel Dulion, Grover Ladd, Martha Noble, Georgie Thomas, Floy Lloyd** (the schoolteacher who gave Nellie a copy of *The Man without A Country*), **Steve Noble** (grandson of his namesake) in front of her, **Willard Ladd** with **Tumsy Noble** in front *(see page 109).*

As the winter approached, however, school attendance fell to 12 or 14; and by Thanksgiving of 1891 there were only five "ladies" remaining in town: Nellie Ladd, Celina Larcine, Mrs. Mullane, Mrs. Miller and Mrs. Nicholson.[47] They celebrated, nevertheless, with chickens, since turkeys had not done well in the climate or the altitude, and they also celebrated New Year's Eve with a party and the White Rock Fife and Drum, who played "national airs" for the occasion.[48]

It was in 1892 as well that townspeople found Doc Boynton at a table in his saloon one morning, having shot himself to death.[52] Doc had said he wanted to start a Denny cemetery, and Grover Ladd said he thought he had succeeded in this by being the (nearly) first one buried there. After his death the distinctive 20 x 50 foot milled lumber building with a double corner entry door and porch first served as a town hall. More mining families stayed in the mining district over the winter of 1892-93, and dances were held in the hall every two weeks. White Rock violinists played there for Christmas Eve and shortly afterwards the Ladds made "Boynton Hall" their home.

Life had its difficult moments and its successes. In February, 1892, there was a flu epidemic, without serious consequences.[49] At one point the snow was so deep and lumber so hard to come by that when a neighbor died there was no way to build a coffin. The Ladds tore up their attic floor boards to give to the grieving family.[50] On the mining front, the Ladd mines were successful, but further exploitation required great effort and financing. In the spring and summer of 1892 the Ladds made a substantial investment in lumber so that Frank could build a flume and begin directing water to the Mountain Boomer for sluicing or what they called "auriferous" (gold) mining. On September 10, Nellie was able to leave with her family, probably for the first time, to go to Chico, returning later that fall.[51]

Fig. 1-14. (Anon.) Nellie Ladd at her third mining district home in "Boynton Hall" in New River City/Denny. c. 1896.

15

Fig. 1-15. (V. Budig-Markin)
Tin pitcher behind Ladd home,
Aug., 2000.

The Douglas fir tree growing up through the porch was small then, but today it is a giant reminder of that home, along with the cellar, now a small depression containing rusty bedsprings, and behind the house a huge pile of evaporated milk cans, enameled metal bowls and pots, a small tin pitcher, and fragments of small bottles and china, some of which probably came from as far as England, like that of the Larcines in Marysville.

Fig. 1-16. (V. Budig-Markin)
Sketch from china fragment
in Marysville, similar to those
behind the Ladd home.

The Ladds' life and standard of living had evolved with the success of Frank's mining ventures. From survival concerns on a mountain slope to a temporary home and active community life, then to the exact center of town. The new Ladd home faced the trail coming up New River, at its intersection with the main street of Denny, which went north to Marysville and White Rock and south to the mines around Slide Creek. After a few short years, the Ladds and their peers lived a quite civilized existence, both in the mining district and beyond it. The community grew to have many central families and businesses and imported many goods from the East coast of the United States and from Europe as well-- Hood's Sarsa Parilla from Lowell, Massachusetts, Dr. Shoop's Family Medicine from Racine, Wisconsin, and sodas of light green glass with heavy rounded bottoms from Belfast, Ireland. Pieces of a bottle of Dr. Kino's New Life Pills (Chicago) near the depression that was the Ladd cellar make one wonder whether Nellie was aware she had terminal cancer when she bought these pills. Traces of Hamlin's Wizard Oil and Lydia E. Pinkham's Vegetable Compound ("a baby in every bottle"[53]), liniment, flavorings and other medicinal concoctions tell their own precious cultural history on vacated sites. *(See page 166, note 27, for information about the laws protecting sites and artifacts on public lands.)*

Fig. 1-17. (V. Budig-Markin)
Similar to green glass round-bottom
bottle fragments found at White Rock, July, 2001.

Fig. 1-18. (Nellie Ladd) Kate Irving (top, second from right)**, her family and friends. Grover Ladd stands far left and the woman with the kerchief may be Alice Jacobs. Annie Irving Wallen, Kate's youngest child, sits on big brother Jim's lap. c. 1912.**

The friendship between the Ladds and the Irvings was enduring, with Frank Ladd and George Irving mining the Hidden Treasure, with Nellie and Kate sharing family stories and their children growing up together. Kate and George's sixth child, born in April, 1893, was named Frank. (The Daileys, who owned the Dailey Ranch about 25 miles down New River, may or may not have named their first daughter Nellie after their friend.) But like so many other mines, the Hidden Treasure played out, and the Irvings moved away, down the 40 miles of the New River to its confluence with the Trinity River at Hawkins Bar. Nellie and Kate and their children traveled back and forth to visit each other for the decades to come. Kate would have 12 surviving children in all.[54]

At their home in November of 1893, the Ladds gave a wedding, "one of the most important events that took place at New River during the past three years," according to the *Trinity Journal* [55] The Ladds were carrying on the "tradition" of their home having been the town hall the year before. "The happy-looking couple," married by the Ladds' friend Justice of the Peace G. W. Brush Yocom, were Carrie Roff, from Cecilville, and Cliff Pharis of East Fork (of the Trinity River).[56]

A new schoolhouse was built in 1894, just when Grover reached school age, seven years old. The new schoolhouse indicated recognition of the increasing number of children who were growing up in the mining community. Classes were canceled when there was no schoolteacher, from 1900 to 1902. Other years school was conducted four months in Denny, after which the teacher moved downstream to Hawkins Bar.[57] The children, too, moved up and downstream with the school, lodging with families there. Grover and Willard finished the eighth grade.[58]

Fig. 1-19. (Nellie Ladd) Grover Ladd and his dog at home by the Christmas tree (left) in front of the American flag. Glass slide. c. 1904.

The November 6, 1894 elections in New River were reported to be scandalous in terms of a large amount of alcohol around the polls. According to reporter "Moses," women's suffrage would prevent such a scene and protect the purity of elections, since the men would not dare act so disgracefully in their presence.[59] Women's suffrage was an important issue to Nellie, who would be among the first women to vote in 1920, as a Democrat, and she would be on the local election committee in Denny. This commitment helps explain the fact that one of the favored elements in the Ladd home decoration was the American flag.

Fig. 1-20. (Nellie Ladd) Friends (including the Irvings) at the dedication of a new mule bridge across the Trinity River. c. 1914.
(See photograph of the bridge on page 137.)

It is hard to picture life in such a rural community, and one tends to picture it as consistently rugged, isolated, and difficult. But the miners did a great deal of business in Weaverville, where they recorded their claims and agreements, in Scott Valley, out of Callahan, where they bought feed for their animals, and in Eureka, San Francisco and Sacramento, where they sought out and met with investors for the mines. Successful miners like Frank sometimes took their families with them. After their first trip to Chico in 1892, the Ladds traveled to visit friends "in the lower country for a few months" in the fall of 1894.[60] Nellie has also left many photographs of local outings with friends.

Amazingly, Grover recollected as well that the family traveled back to Maine when the boys were very young.[61] They went to visit the family, to let Willard, the talkative child, and Grover, with his quiet sense of humor, get to know their paternal family there. The *Trinity Journal* reported many activities of the Ladd family in 1898, when Frank Ladd, Sr. came to visit from Maine for the summer. Returning to the East Coast, Frank Sr. went through Chico, where he met another son, who lived there and who accompanied him home. *(See also page 100.)*

Fig. 1-21. (Nellie Ladd) Hollyhocks in the Larcine home fireplace. c. 1900.

Life was getting easier, at least in terms of standard of living, and Nellie Ladd began her amateur photography career. She was among those who first used simple Kodak cameras. For the next 25 years, she recorded cultural and mining history, playful encounters, and arranged settings and portraits. Using both glass slides and negatives, she developed her photographs herself. She saved her work carefully, as did her son Grover after her death.

Family friends still have a few of the Ladd possessions. Smokey Bergstrom, living in the new Denny today, has their carved dresser and oval mirror frame hauled up to Old Denny by mule and then back down again when the Ladds moved to the new Denny in 1921. He has a Ladd trunk, made of tin-coated board lined with designed paper, containing a lacy camisole and house linens *(see page 144)*. And he has given the author books with Nellie's signature *(see cover)* and others with inscriptions to her from friends. She had a mountain flower book, several California State School Series readers, a carpentry encyclopedia she gave to Willard in 1907, novels *20,000 Leagues under the Sea* and *The Man without a Country (see page 27)* and she kept a picture of the Pope.

**Fig. 1-22.
(Nellie Ladd)
Denny Store.
c. 1910.**
Glass slide.

The Ladds purchased the Denny Store in 1894, according to Grover. His account of the date of the purchase, which conflicts with others (1896 or 1897), makes sense because this year marked the waning of the mining boom. The Brizard Store in White Rock was sold about this time as well. So it was that Frank stopped mining full-time and became a part-time storekeeper, maintaining the name "Denny Store" and Post Office. Like the Ladd home, the store was built of lumber milled locally. The interior, both down- and upstairs, was rip-sawed sugar pine. Merchandise was sold in the front room of the store and liquor in the back. Grover said much later that the whiskey, stored in ten-gallon kegs, was sold in shots bigger than those today, for ten cents a shot.[62] *(See story, page 102.)*

21

Grover and Willard used the old store account ledgers left from the Denny Store to practice their penmanship, write grammar lessons, copy poems and songs, write about their hunts and the weather.

Using available space on the ledger pages, they recorded addresses of their father's relatives in Maine and, later, those of the local girls as they moved away. For more than two decades they wrote their intimate overlay on the business records of the community, telling of "a nice day," hoping it would last. They wrote of "troubadours," of America, "the human heart's a seasoned violin," Texas and Manhattan, mine tunnels they dug in winter, "getting down a set of timbers," "mucking awhile," and hunting with other "young fellows."

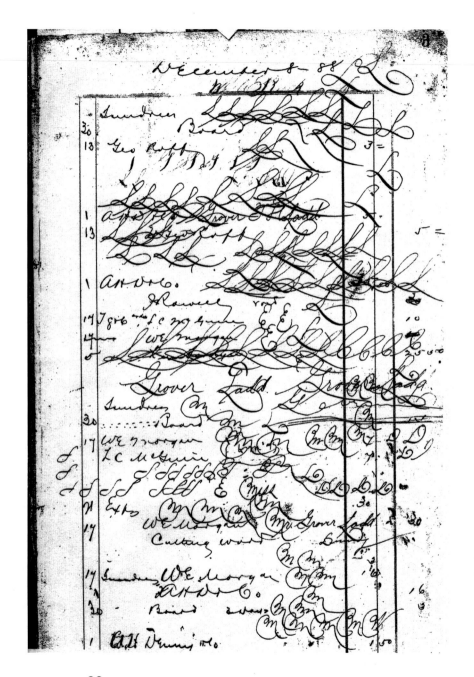

Fig. 1-23. Page from Denny Store ledger (1888) with Grover practicing his penmanship many years later.

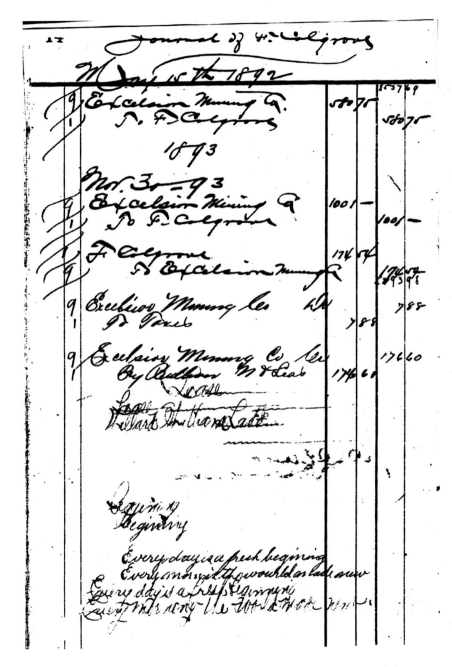

It is Willard who copied the lines from the poem "Every day is a fresh beginning" on an 1892-1893 journal.

Another lesson of one of the boys, perhaps Willard, proposes adjectives for certain nouns, giving a sense of the boys' frame of mind and level of linguistic preparation, perhaps as they approached the eighth grade:

> "retentive memory
> becoming hat
> faithful friend
> tiresome journey
> lucious (sic) peach
> blustering wind
> poisonous serpent
> amiable disposition,
> gorgous (sic) sunset."

In a much later store ledger Grover, Willard and Frank Patten kept a winter diary while digging a tunnel for the Gun Barrel Mine *(see map, page 7).* Frank wrote that he was "still recovering from a coon hunt."

Fig. 1-24. Accounts in journal of F. Colgrove[63] (1892) over which Willard wrote his name and lines of a poem.

23

One of Nellie Ladd's early photographs portrays the boys studying at the table at home. The flowery wallpaper and tablecloth would probably have been Nellie's contribution to the home decor, since a saloon would most likely not have looked this domestic or feminine.

Fig. 1-25. (Nellie Ladd) Willard and Grover studying at home. c.1900.

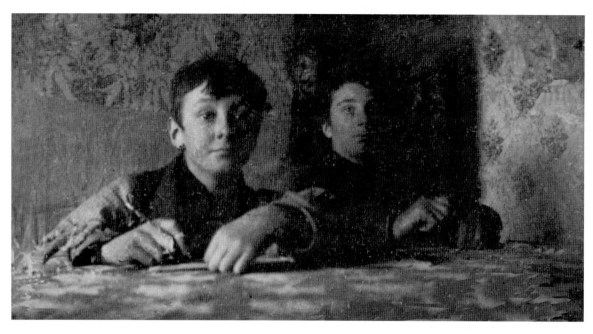

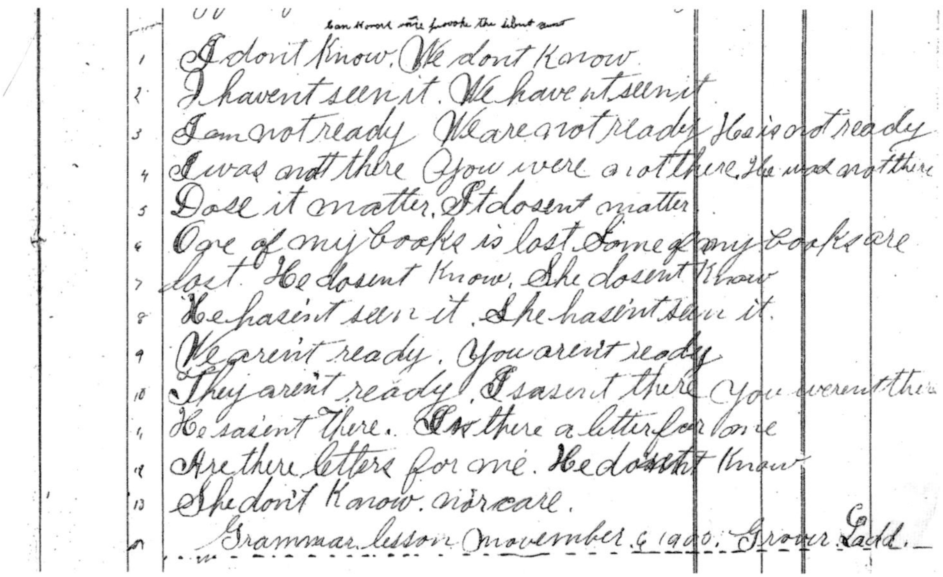

I dont know. We dont know.
I havent seen it. We havent seen it.
I am not ready. We are not ready. He is not ready
I was not there. You were not there. He was not there
Dose it matter. It dosent matter.
One of my books is lost. Some of my books are
lost. He dosent know. She dosent know
He hasent seen it. She hasent seen it.
We arent ready. You arent ready
They arent ready. I wasent there. You werent there
He wasent there. Is there a letter for me
Are there letters for me. He dosent know
She dont know. nor care.
Grammar lesson November 6 1900. Grover Ladd.

One of Grover's grammar lessons, recorded in available space in old store ledgers, gives irregular verb forms and negative contractions. This exercise was written during the period when Floy Lloyd was the boys' teacher *(see page 14)*.

Fig. 1-26. Grover's grammar lesson Nov. 6, 1905, copied in a store ledger.

Fig. 1-27. (Nellie Ladd) Willard's first bear. c. 1903.

A long with the local mines, Nellie's favorite photographic subjects were her two boys. Grover and Willard were hunters, and she captured their proud successes. She photographed their chores, their skiing, their leisure time at home, their animals, their mining activities, their pack train, their friends. They remained close to their mother, traveling with her and writing back to her when out of town alone. Notice the foreground focus and a soft swirling background around the central figures.

Fig. 1-28. (Nellie Ladd) Postcard picturing snow, icicles, trees and a snow-covered cabin. 1910.

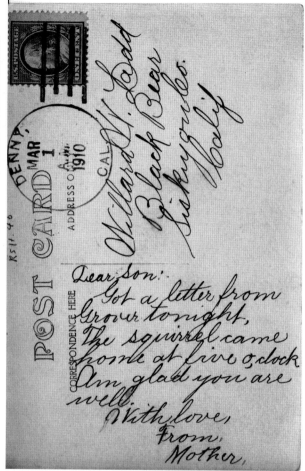

Dear Son:
Got a letter from Grover tonight. The squirrel came home at five o'clock. Am glad you are well.
With love,
from,
Mother.

Willard W. Ladd
Black Bear
Siskiyou Co.
Cal.

Fig. 1-29. (Nellie Ladd) Address side of postcard sent by Nellie to her son Willard in Black Bear. March 1, 1910.

Nellie made and sold postcards in the Denny Store and sent and received them herself. Blank postcards were part of the photographic "outfits" sold by different companies, including Sears *(see page 38)*. The snow scene photograph with icicles and a snow-covered roof is clearly an amateur image, yet extraordinary for its time, locale, and postcard format. Rare written words from mother to son are captured on the reverse. 23 days later, a postcard from Grover postmarked in Black Bear, was sent to his parents with this message: "Here is hoping we will be with you Easter morning. Your son, Grover H. Ladd."[64] Two other 1910 Easter greeting postcards are part of a collection of 105 postcards of the Ladds owned by Rich Lorenz and shared with Gay Berrien and the author in May of 2003. Another, written Feb. 6, 1911 from San Francisco, is a valentine with doves, forget-me-nots, and an arrow with "To My Valentine." The inscription of the card addressed to "Mrs. Frank Ladd," though unsigned, is most likely from her husband Frank: "With all sweet wishes to my <u>Valentine</u>."[65]

The Ladds' writing and reading give us an intimate look at their life. Our earliest evidence of Nellie's writing, recognizable from her signature *(see cover)*, is the designation "New River 1887" in an 1886 (copyright) edition of *The Farm and Household Cyclopædia: A Complete Ready Reference Liberary for Farmers, Gardeners, Fruit Growers, Stockmen and Housekeepers, Containing a Large Fund of Useful Information, Facts, Hints and Suggestions, in the Various Departments of Agriculture, Horticulture, Live Stock Raising, Poultry Keeping, Bee Keeping, Dairy Farming, Fertilizers, Rural Architecture, Farm Implements, Household Management, Domestic Affairs, Cookery, Ladies' Fancy Work, Floriculture, Medical Matters, Etc., Etc., with Two Hundred and Forty-Nine Illustrations.*[66] There are stains in the chapters of "Cooking Recipes," "The Home Physician," and "Rural Architecture" ("The Complete Stock Barn"), and a bookmark in the chapter "The Poultry Yard." The page marker is a humorous song titled "When You've Got Money (You've Got Friends)," cut from newspaper or magazine print. There are many little dash marks, perhaps made by a child.

A 1908 postcard from Nellie in Chico to her husband in Denny reads, "Dear Frank, Got letter from the boys yesterday. It is trying to storm here. I am well. With Love, Nell. E. Ladd." On another, written one Easter, Nellie writes home, "This reminds me of the pussy willows you and the boys always bring in spring. And is always a pleasure to me. Your loving wife, Nellie."[67]

Grover had a book by Mara Pratt, *The Fairyland of Flowers* (1890), in which he wrote his name in childish hand. Part of a Boston educational series, The Young Folks' Library of Choice Literature, it included educational tracing exercises for plant identification. Marking the review lesson pages was a revenue stamp from a bottle of Piso's Remedy cough medicine and cure for catarrh. A child has scribbled all over both sides of the one-inch revenue stamp *(right)*.

Willard left a book inscribed to him by Nellie, "Presented by Mrs. E. E. Ladd to Willard W. Ladd, Jan. 17, 1911," his 22nd birthday, the *Encyclopedia of Carpentry and Contracting: A Complete Manual of Carpentry and Joinery, Covering Every Known Detail of the Trade ::::: Designed to Afford Practical Help in the Every-Day Problems of the Carpenter, the Builder and the Architect.*[68] Willard, Grover, Frank and family friend Frank Patten had built the arrastra and buildings at the Gun Barrel Mine in 1906 and 1907.

Fig. 1-30. (Nellie Ladd-- with cropping by her boys) Rose Ryan. c. 1899.

Grover and Willard grew up and became handsome young men. From adolescents in homely attire cutting out the face of their sweetheart Rose from their mother's photograph, they began to dress elegantly and visit with their friend on the porch with their parents and their dogs. They usually posed with her together. Nellie took one photograph of Grover, Rose and Willard from an angle below the group, emphasizing Rose's skirt and the joyful gait of the apparently carefree and sophisticated threesome.

In a store ledger, the boys noted down a San Francisco address for Rose in 1906. In Fig. 1-31 she may have been dressing for the city, in preparation for her departure from Denny in 1905 or 1906.

Fig. 1-31. (Nellie Ladd) Rose Ryan and her two beaux. c. 1905.

28

Grover and Willard grew up with the Irving children. They lodged with each other over the years to go to school in good weather (Denny) and bad (Hawkins Bar) and visited each other frequently. As young adults they seem to have been a warm and gracious generation. They wrote and dressed well, danced and partied with their families, and helped Nellie set up stylish group photographs.

Fig. 1-32. (Nellie Ladd) (L-R) Ted Irving, Blanche Irving, unknown, Bill Gray, Roy Irving, and young Kate Irving. c. 1917.

29

In 1902 Nellie was appointed Denny Post Office clerk. She participated in the school board and the election board, even before women could vote. She and Frank offered lodging to young people from out of the area who wanted to go to school at the Denny school. The 1900 Census reports Laura Noble, 16, boarding with the Ladds, as well as the schoolteacher, Bessie Coady (aged 24). *See Appendix B: 1900 U. S. Census.*

Nellie's photography recorded the minor dramas of her community, from the frolicking of the two bear cubs adopted from the wild to "Mrs. Brown and her short skirt" as she posed on what may have been the tramway of the Mountain Boomer Mine. She stands on the ore car rails.

Nellie photographed her women friends--and sometimes handed them the camera as well--at the Tener Camp, at the Boomer, on a horseback excursion to Mary Blaine Meadow *(see page 95)*, on her porch hammock, in a group sitting on the grass, in the fork of a large tree. As her boys grew up she seems to have had time to enjoy herself and visit different places, but she mostly photographed the sights and people of her own community.

Fig. 1-33. (Nellie Ladd) "Mrs. Brown and her short skirt." c. 1907. Self-titled.

Other *Trinity Journal* and *Blue Lake Advocate* news relevant to the Ladd family history over the years:

1892 In New River, "Politics is the order of the day. Free trade, tariff reform, and protection...controversies... Columbus Day...The floating of the stars and stripes...was the only thing remarkable to characterize the 400th anniversary of the discovery of America...the great political storm of 1892." *Trinity Journal*, 10/29/1892.

1898 Frank Ladd's father, Frank Ladd, Sr., came to visit for several months from Maine. (*Trinity Journal* articles)

1900 --Nellie gave a supper, "a success in every way," following the New River Grange Grand March and ball. Pickles seemed to have been popular. *Trinity Journal*, 6/9/19.

--"...the best showing I have ever seen on the Boomer...good ledge...the Hard Tack." *Trinity Journal*, 1/20/1900.

1901 Denny population: 16. *Trinity Journal,*, 8/24/1901.

1902 Nellie and Frank hosted an election in their home. *Trinity Journal,*, 10/4/1902.[69]

1903 --Nellie took a trip alone for a "visit" to San Francisco. *Trinity Journal*, 9/5/1903.

--Frank Ladd and Frank Patten struck a good prospect on Emigrant Creek. *Trinity Journal*, 9/5/1903.

1904 Frank Ladd selected to be elections inspector. *Trinity Journal*, 10/1/1904.

1908 --"The Ladd brothers are running a tunnel on their ledge at the head of Eagle Creek." *Trinity Journal*, 8/1/1908.

--"The Ladd pack train arrived today from Korbel with twenty-four packs of general merchandise for Mr. Ladd." "New River Items," from the *Blue Lake Advocate*, *Trinity Journal*, 10/10/1908.

1911 --Nellie Ladd, Celina Larcine, and Mrs. Charles ("Jakie") Jacobs spent the day at the Hunter Mine. *Trinity Journal*, 9/23/1911.

--"The women throughout this section ("Lower Trinity") are very happy over the fact of woman suffrage carrying the day and feel very grateful to the men who voted for the cause." *Trinity Journal*, 11/4/1911.

--Frank Ladd testified in Superior Court for a case involving two friends, Mr. Dailey and Mr. Irving. On his way Frank saw his first "motor car" and rode in it from North Fork (Helena) to Weaverville. *Trinity Journal*, 6/26/1915.

1915 --Willard Ladd was fire guard on the Mary Blaine and mining the Gun Barrel. Grover was in charge of the family pack train. Because of the advent of parcel post, the pack train was shortened to 16 mules, carrying objects "forbidden by our Uncle" (Sam). *Trinity Journal,* 6/26/1915.

--The Cowens from Quimby visited the Ladds for two days. Mrs. Ladd went back with them as far as Tener's and spent the day visiting with Mrs. Brown (Clara Moore). *Trinity Journal*, 6/3/1915. From the *Blue Lake Advocate*.

1916 Mrs. Brown (Clara Moore) and Mr. Pettry came up from the Tener Camp and went to the Mary Blaine. Mrs. Brown visited with Mrs. Ladd and was to leave for Eureka for a month. *Trinity Journal*, 8/12/1916.

1917 World War I: Grover and Willard Ladd registered for the draft at the Denny post office. *Trinity Journal*, 6/16/1917.

1918 --Grover and Willard went to Eureka to enlist, "hoping to make the trip to France together." *Trinity Journal*, 2/23/1918. (Willard rose to the rank of Corporal in the 319th Corps of Engineers. Grover did not join the Army.)

--Grover and Willard were on Grand Honor Roll of Trinity Co. for purchase of war bonds. *Trinity Journal,* 1/3/1918.

Nellie Ladd wrote a distinctive obituary in the *Trinity Journal* for her friend Celina Larcine, "the first white woman in the New River mining camp." The obituary tells a dramatic story about Celina's daughter at the age of eleven in a confrontation with yellow jackets and another humorous story about Celina and a man named Pony Brown. *(See page 96.)* The article ends with a lyrical eulogy:

"Do what we may, we cannot suppress the awe and faith which the heart will breathe and utter, and none so hardened, journeying the pathway of life, that they can stay the tears which well forth as they behold--

The milestones into headstones changed,
'Neath every one a friend."[70]

--Nellie Ladd

Fig. 1-34.
(Nellie Ladd)
Peter and
Celina Larcine
in their home.
Glass plate.
c. 1906.

By 1920 Nellie and Frank Ladd were the last two residents of "old Denny." Even their children had moved down to the "new" Denny to homestead for the family. Well known for their store and their warm welcome--"Mr. and Mrs. Ladd are still at the old store and are always glad to see any old friend who may drop in"[71]-- Frank and Nellie Ladd finally closed up shop and left town in 1921. *See Frank at the Denny Store in uly, 1920, page 100.)* It was a long last trip down-river, since Nellie had terminal rectal cancer that would end her life on February 10, 1922, on her 63rd birthday, according to her obituary.

Nellie was remembered for her community spirit, kindness and generosity. "Her hospitality was enjoyed by nearly everyone who traveled from afar to that secluded nook of Trinity, and her kindness, which knew no bounds, was heralded far and wide."[70] She had many women friends her age and photographed many young women as well. Her self-portrait with Kate Irving's daughter Belle tells the story of Nellie's closeness to the new generation of women to grow up in Trinity County.

Fig. 1-35. (Nellie Ladd--self-portrait)
Nellie and Belle Irving. c. 1910.

NOTES
CHAPTER I

1. Information about Nellie Ladd's birth, death, years in California (48) and in her place of death (36) are taken from her death certificate at the Trinity County (CA) courthouse. The information is not all reconcilable and thus contains errors. The previous marriage information comes from an article in the *Trinity Journal*, Frank Ladd's obituary: "Frank J. Ladd and Elizabeth Ellen Graham were united in marriage in San Francisco in 1886." Nellie's given name was actually Ellen Elizabeth Casey. The 1900 Census *(see Appendix B)* suggests she had a child (deceased) from her first marriage.

Nellie Ladd's place of birth has been researched by Gay Berrien, who discovered in Portsmouth, NH both the child (Ellen Elizabeth Casey) and her mother (also Ellen Casey), with the daughter's birthdate of Feb. 10, 1859, exactly a year earlier than previously thought. A year later the family disappeared from the records, suggesting a move, perhaps to Massachusetts, where Nellie said she was born. There was no record in Massachusetts of the birth of an Ellen E. Casey. The author selected this research as the correct information and as the reason for the nickname "Nellie," to distinguish her from her mother.

2. The *Trinity Journal* first reported the find Sept. 30, 1882 (from New River, 9/17/1882): "F. M. Kerby and Mr. Sherwood found some very rich croppings last June and with very little trouble discovered the ledge from which they came...still another was found by a man--O. Clement..." By the next summer the New River news from May 26 includes Frank Ladd: "Ladd & Clement are now at work putting up an arastra on the 'Mountain Boomer.'" (6/9/1883)

3. "New River Letter," *Trinity Journal*, Feb. 21, 1885: "Next is the Mountain Boomer, one of the first locations made in the District. As luck would have it, Frank Ladd, an energetic and go-ahead fellow, got one-third interest to put up an arastra. The ledge is small, rather broken, yet tolerably well defined. Their arastra ran from about the first of June to the latter end of October. I am positive the rock crushed paid over $100 per ton. The partners had a kick and work was suspended in October. It is natural, you know, for some men to belly-ache and kick."

4. See note 3.

5. Grover Ladd's recollections are recorded in Gay Holland's obituary, "Grover Ladd, Pioneer of New River Area, Succombs," *Trinity Journal*, January, 1973.

6. "New River Mining District and the Route by Which It Is Reached," *Trinity Journal,* Jan. 10, 1885.

7. "New River Mines," *Trinity Journal,* Nov. 22, 1884; and "The Coming Boom: The New River Mining District," *Trinity Journal,* Dec. 13, 1884.

8. "New River District," Trinity Journal, Jan. 3, 1885. The trail was built by Smith B. Brooks, who had located the Mary Blaine, White Elephant and Brooks mines.

9. "The Coming Boom: The New River Mining District," *Trinity Journal,* Dec. 13, 1884.

10. Florence E. Morris, "Upper New River: A Tale of Three Cities," *Trinity 1970,* p. 22; Holland, "Grover Ladd," 1973.

11. Dogbane (*Apocynum*) is also called "Indian hemp." Its strong stems were used by native American peoples to make rope and string for weaving mats and baskets, fishing and carrying nets. Cords made from its leaves were made into rope, nets, camping bags and snares.

12. Such was the fate of travelers described by missionary women Mary Elliott and Mabel Reed in the Klamath Valley about thirty miles to the north of the New River mines: *In the Land of the Grasshopper Song: Two Women in the Klamath River Indian Country in 1908-09* (Lincoln and London: Univ. of Nebraska Press, 1957). The Frank Irving story comes from Gay Holland Berrien, "The Wallen Ranch and the Irving Family of Hawkin's Creek, " *Trinity 1996*, publication of the Trinity County Historical Society, Weaverville, CA, p. 43.

13. A. L. Kroeber, *Handbook of the Indians of California* (New York: Dover Publications, 1976). Bulletin 78. Reprint.

14. James Bauman, "Chimariko placenames and the boundaries of Chimariko territory," *American Indian and Indoeuropean Studies Papers in Honor of Madison S. Beeler.* Ed. K. Klar, M. Langdon, S. Silver (The Hague, Paris, New York: Mouton Publishers, 1980), pp. 13-29; Shirley Silver, "Chimariko," *Handbook of North American Indians,* ed. William C. Sturtevant (Washington, D. C.: Smithsonian Institution, 1978), vol. 8: California, ed. Robert F. Heizer, 205-210.

15. Bauman, 1980; Doris Carroll, "Bill Noble," *Trinity Journal,* March 18, 1970.

16. Gay Holland Berrien, conversation March 6, 2002; Berrien, "New River and Some of Its First Settlers," *Trinity 1998,* p. 63.

17. Bauman, 1980; Silver, 1978; Kroeber, 1976 (reprint); Janet P. Eidsness, *Prehistoric Archeology within Chimariko Territory, Northwest California,* Master's Thesis, Sonoma State University, 1985. Both Margaret A. Wooden, Trinity and Humboldt County historian, and Gay Berrien, in her unpublished article"Native Americans in New River at White Contact (1851),"explain that the Southern Hupa, the Tsnungwe, claim territory up the South Fork of the Trinity and into New River. Berrien concludes: "Because of the present politics involved with tribes competing for Federal monies and jockeying for Federal recognition, three tribes (other than the Chimariko and the New River Shasta)--Karuk, Hupa, and Tsnungwe-- are claiming parts of New River as their ancestral ground. There are no living Chimariko or New River Shasta around today to question this!"

18. Linguist J. P. Harrington spent time with Sally Noble and photographed her. This photocopy of a photograph may have come originally from Harrington, via Berrien. Harrington's archives are located in Santa Barbara, CA and at the Smithsonian Institution. See Bauman, 1980.

19. Morris, "Three Cities," p. 31.

20. Shirley Silver, "Shastan Peoples," *Handbook of North American Indians,* ed. William C. Sturtevant (Washington, D. C.: Smithsonian Institution, 1978), vol. 8: California, ed. Robert F. Heizer, 211-224. See also Vivian Tye (granddaughter of Setti Jim), "Where Have All the Indians Gone?" *Trinity 1970,* 37-47. According to Kroeber, quoted by others, the population of New River Shasta was from 200 to 300 at White contact; that of the Chimariko was similar.

21. Silver, 1978: 205, 222 (from two different chapters).

22. Conflicting accounts accord the attacks to local vs. an outside group from Siskiyou County, to the north. See also Berrien, unpublished article, "Native Americans in New River at White Contact (1851)," March, 2002.23. "New River," *Trinity Journal,* June 17, 1882.

23. *Trinity Journal,* June 17, 1882.

24. Gay Holland, transcribed "Conversation with Grover Ladd," 1965.

25. "The New River Mines," *Trinity Journal,* Jan. 17, 1885 reported that at Francis, 20 miles down New River, "They buy about six thousand dollars worth of gold dust at the store..., twenty-eight hundred from Chinamen and thirty-two from white men..."

26. Taylor D. Robertson. "The Chinese in Trinity County--1865," *Trinity 1970,* p. 15, from his Master's dissertation: "There were three known Joss Houses in Trinity County, two in Weaverville and one in Lewiston Chinatown. "Joss" is pidgin English to describe idol or deity and is a corruption of the Portuguese word, "Deos" or God. In the 16th century Portuguese explorers applied the word "Deos" to East Indian Oriental idols. Today one Joss House remains in Weaverville and is still being used by a local family. This Joss House is now a California State Historical Monument."

27. "Trinity's Census," *Trinity Journal,* Jan. 10, 1891; Robertson, "The Chinese in Trinity County," p. 17: "By 1900, only 336 Chinese remained in the county. Many of the remaining Chinese had turned to cooking and gardening and laundry work, finding employment at the hotels, mining camps and residences throughout the county. In some mines they were employed as ordinary laborers...gardening...three Chinese mining areas...: China Bar on New River (*Trinity Journal,* 4/21/1960), China Bar above Lewiston... and China Gulch near the Chinese cemetery at the north end of Weaverville (*Trinity 1956*)...China Slide..."

28. *White Rock Archeological Site, F. S. Site 05-14-54-177, Trinity County, California,* p. 86.

29. Gay Holland Berrien, conversation with the author during summer 2001 expedition after locating the Ridgeway Mine.

30. Morris, "Three Cities," p. 23 plus many articles in the *Trinity Journal.* Known as Captain Jim (J. C.) Frantz, Frantzen, Franz, and Franzen, the Trinity Co. Great Registers list him as James Christian Franzen (p. 169).

31. San Francisco *Evening Post,* Jan. 2, 1885; reprinted by the *Trinity Journal,* Jan. 10, 1885 and by the *Mining & Scientific Press,* Jan. 24, 1885, p. 53.

32. The buildings were enumerated in "Jock," "New River Letter," *Trinity Journal,* April 25, 1885. See also Morris, "Three Cities," p. 23.

33. Holland, "Grover Ladd," 1973.

34. "Permanent camp" of 500: *Trinity Journal,* April 24, 1886. See also Morris, "Three Cities." Population 300 "some 35 years ago" (1886): *Trinity Journal,* March 5, 1921.

35. "Officers of Election," *Trinity Journal,* Oct. 9, 1886.

36. "New River,: *Trinity Journal,* July 2, 1887. The new ledge discovery was reported the day after Grover was born.

37. In Nellie Ladd's tribute to Celina Larcine upon her death, she told the story of the Larcines' move to New River in 1884, which is recounted in Chapter IV, "Local Characters and Stories," page 96.

38. Both the decision to hire the doctor and news of the hire appeared in "New River Items," *Trinity Journal,* April 21, 1888.

39. Gay Holland Berrien, "The Wallen Ranch and the Irving Family of Hawkin's Creek," *Trinity 1996,* pp. 40, 64.

40. A. E. Yocom, "New River Heard From: Nineteen Feet of Snow and More Falling, Loss of Life and Accidents," *Humboldt Times,* March 1, 1890.

41. See note 40.

42. Berrien, conversation Jan. 10, 2000.

43. "Returned," *Trinity Journal,* March 1, 1890.

44. Dean Swift quoted in "New River Letter," *Trinity Journal,* Feb. 7, 1885.

45. *Trinity Journal,* Sept. 13, 1890.

46. "Aunty," "From New River," *Trinity Journal,* Aug. 29, 1891.

47. "New River Items," *Trinity Journal,* Oct. 31, 1891; "New River," *Trinity Journal,* Nov. 28, 1891.

48. "Friendly," "New River Items," *Trinity Journal,* March 12, 1892.

49. See note 48.

50. The story of the coffin was reported by Berrien during the 2001 expedition to the New River mine district in July, 2001. When Grover told her the story, he was not sure of the year of the event.

51. "Moses," "New River Items," *Trinity Journal,* Sept. 24, 1892.

52. Berrien, conversation Jan. 2000.

53. Yvonne Lillehaug remembers her mother saying (North Dakota, 1920s) that her own mother (New York, 1900s) always told her this was true. Her mother-in-law Marie Budig (Colorado, 1940s), moreover, told her that her own two daughters were the result of taking the compound after not having been able to conceive. Pat Craig, Trinity County resident and research expedition regular, remembers the same saying (Massachusetts, 1930s).

54. Berrien, "Wallen Ranch," 1996.

55. "A Friend," "New River," *Trinity Journal,* Nov. 18, 1893.

56. See note 55.

57. Entire paragraph from Berrien, conversation Jan., 2000.

58. Holland, "Grover Ladd," 1973.

59. "Moses," "New River Items," *Trinity Journal,* Nov. 17, 1894.

60. *Trinity Journal,* Sept. 8, 1894.

61. Holland, "Grover Ladd," 1973..

62. Gay Holland, "The Denny Store in 1912," *Trinity Journal,* Jan. 19, 1972.

63. Frank Colgrove operated the Excelsior Mine. He also owned a ranch near Callahan where the Ladds bought feed and other supplies.

64. Transcripts, Ladd family postcard collection, Rich Lorenz.

65. Transcripts, Ladd family postcard collection, Rich Lorenz.

66. *The Farm and Household Cyclopædia* (NY: Lupton, Pub., 1885).

67. Transcripts, Ladd family postcard collection, Rich Lorenz.

68. Fred T. Hodgson, ed., *Encyclopedia of Carpentry and Contracting* (Chicago, Minneapolis, New York: Cree Publishing Co., 1903).

69. The election board included election judges G. W. Brush Yocom and F. M. King, inspectors E. O. Nelson and D. P. Lamberson, clerks Christopher Ramsett and E. A. Piersol, and ballot clerks Alex Boyd and L. J. Brown.

70. Nellie Ladd, "Death of Mrs. Larcine," *Trinity Journal,* Mar. 13, 1915

71. "Items of Interest from Denny and Vicinity," *Trinity Journal,* Nov. 20, 1915.

72. "Mrs. Ellen Ladd of Denny Passes Over the Great Divide," *Trinity Journal,* Feb. 25, 1922.

CHAPTER II

Nellie Ladd, the Photographer

Nellie Ladd's amateur photographic career began in about 1895, around the time she and Frank bought the Denny store and post office next door. Grover and Willard were in school, about eight and six years old. Grover remembered that his mother learned the arts of photography and developing on her own, experimenting with different equipment over the years.[1] Many of her early prints have deteriorated, but some of her glass slides have remained in remarkable condition. Her first photographs reflect interests in the framing of subjects and, in particular, framing by means of a fading "fog effect" around the object. In about 1900 or 1902, she became more serious about photographing places, events and people that defined the New River mining district. Then, around 1913, after the establishment of the Tener placer mining operation and its community at Robber's Roost, Nellie photographed more of the process of mining, while at the same time capturing beautiful snow scenes juxtaposing white snow and dark buildings. The photographer was especially attentive to sunlight and the many effects of water on landscape. Images of power appear frequently in Ladd's photographs of working people and animals, rivers, machinery, and rock, while other very different shots accentuate a contrasting softness, intimacy, simplicity and beauty of daily life.

We have no information today about the specific camera equipment the photographer used, other than the products of her work--the glass plates, the negatives and the prints, including matted prints. Necessarily a practical woman, photography also gave Nellie an outlet for her artistic sensibilities. She began to take photographs, to learn and practice basic techniques in photography, such as the framing of subjects and the creation of a fog effect, while recording precious memories.

Fig. 2-1. (V. Budig-Markin) Sears glass plate camera, 1900.

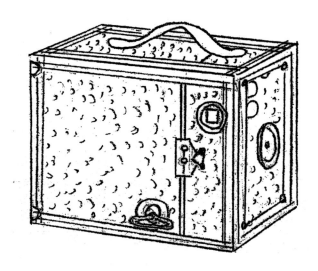

Fig. 2-2. (V. Budig-Markin) A "family" camera given away by *The American Woman* **in a 1917 promotion.**

We know that by 1895 Kodak cameras were popular with men and women amateur photographers.[2] A copy of *Collier's* magazine from May 1900, found in Denny had an amateur photogaphy contest for photos of Yellowstone National Park. The fall 1900 Sears catalogue offered two cameras and photographic "outfits," both including camera, tripod, case, developing trays, solutions, plates, paste brush, darkroom lamp, plates, card mounts, paper, intensifier, hypo for fixing negatives or prints, photo mounting paste, focus cloth, and instruction book. The less expensive camera had a single or double "rapid rectilinear lens" and the more expensive a "double valve unicum shutter" opening either as long as the bulb was pressed or time release with two squeezes of the bulb (one to open, a second to close).[3] Plates came in 5" x 7", 6 1/2" x 8" and 8" x 10". A later copy of the *American Woman* (1917) gave "outing" and "family" cameras to subscribers for ten and fourteen new subscriptions to the magazine, respectively.

38

An advertisement by the Chicago Ferrotype Co. in a 1914 copy of *Woman's World* found in Denny even shows a woman holding its one-minute Mandel-ette camera, a camera without plates or film producing finished photographs or postcards in one minute.

Women in particular were offered money-making, enjoyable hobbies in photography, with supplies and instructions by mail. Companies stressed the fact that no previous experience was necessary. The 1914 and 1917 magazines reflected the new roles of women during the First World War.

Earn Money in Spare Time

making one minute photos of your neighbors, friends, etc. Loads of fun besides. Pleasant diversion—delightful work.

The Mandel-ette A One Minute Camera, makes finished pictures on post cards in a minute's time. No Films, Plates or Dark Room. Just snap the button—in one minute you see the picture. No Experience needed. No trouble or fuss—but real picture-taking joys. Write for booklet. Free.

THE CHICAGO FERROTYPE CO.
A310 Ferrotype Bldg. or A310 Public Bk. Bldg.
Chicago   New York

Fig. 2-3. Advertisement in *Woman's World*, Chicago, 1914.

Fig. 2-4. (Nellie Ladd) The Ladd home and boys in Denny. c. 1895.
Matted photograph. Approx. original size.

The early "fog-effect" photographs vary widely in subject matter. They generally reflect concern with framing, focus, the play of light, geometric design, and balance. Some of these photographs have deteriorated in the last century. A tiny photograph of the Ladd home may have been among the earliest photographs taken in Old Denny. Other small matted photographs were clearly focused, like the photograph of Steve Noble's mule Rosa, taken much later.

Fig. 2-5. (Nellie Ladd) Steve Noble's mule Rosa. c. 1905.
Matted photograph. Approx. original size.

39

Fig. 2-6. (Nellie Ladd) Willard and Grover Ladd
hanging and skinning their deer. c. 1898.

Fig. 2-7. (Nellie Ladd) Grover and Willard Ladd
splitting wood. c. 1900.

Nellie photographed the successful hunts of Grover and Willard--coyotes, deer, bobcats, and bears--and practiced lighting and framing techniques in early photographs of the boys with their game *(see page 25)*. In Fig. 2-6 they are in the process of skinning a hung deer. The frame from which the deer is hung becomes the artistic frame of the photograph, as do the natural poses of the boys. In Fig. 2-7, they are splitting firewood or shingles. In both shots the photographer tells the story of the life of her family in a mining camp using careful composition, but the later wood-splitting photograph is more complex, incorporating action, light and camera angle more successfully than its earlier counterpart. Notice the ax handle to the right in Fig. 2-7, its head dark against the light, while its light-colored handle contrasts with the dark post behind it. Meanwhile, the ax to the left points to the boys at the center of the photograph and focuses the spectator's attention on the action as the silhouetted boys seem to alternate hitting the splitting wedge in the wood with a maul.

Fig. 2-8. (Nellie Ladd) North Fork (Helena). c. 1900.

Nellie also used neighboring communities as subject matter for such photographs. One was a scene from North Fork (of the Trinity), now Helena, on the Trinity River. New River residents passed through North Fork on their way from Weaverville to Denny, either north up to East Fork, Rattlesnake and Grizzly, or continuing along the Trinity, heading up the New River at Hawkins Bar *(see area sketch, page 3)*. The composition subordinates people to environment and construction. The softened light adds a romantic atmosphere. Most of the fog effect photographs mark domesticated environments.

41

Fig. 2-9. (Nellie Ladd)
The rocking chair.
c. 1905.

The atmosphere created by the use of filtered natural light, the interplay of angles and curves, and the soft focus of the rocking chair photograph suggest a growing sophistication of technique. Subtle textures are juxtaposed, from the small designs on the translucent curtain panel to the carpet under the chair and the soft fabric seat cushion. Light and shadow cover the full range of shades from white to black. The points of light on the fold of curtain at the lower left corner of the window are nearly impressionistic, while other folds give a soft line of light guiding the eye toward the center of the photograph. Other elements also guide the eye into the photograph: the bolster or bed corner, the chair rockers, and the angles of the ceiling and the window frame.

Some of the most touching photographs of the Nellie Ladd collection feature her two handsome sons, who were quite photogenic. Grover and Willard had many interests and abilities, worked hard, and were surrounded by their animals. The family often had three dogs at a time, and they appear in photographs inside, as well as outside, the home and almost always near the boys. The horses and mules had names and were well cared for. But these were work animals, and their work depended on their good health, which was the responsibility of the boys. The mules of the pack train had to be boarded at Callahan over the winter and brought back again in late May. Hay, too, had to be brought in from Scott Valley for the livestock. Meanwhile, Grover and Willard had to complete their schooling, either at home with their mother or at school in Denny or down at Hawkins Bar. As young men, Grover and Willard worked the Gun Barrel Mine with their father and Frank Patten. In the winter of 1907 they dug a tunnel for the mine for over a month, recording their work in an old store ledger.

Fig. 2-10. (Nellie Ladd) Willard and Grover with Skip and pups on the porch. c.1903.

43

The water-and-work landscapes exploit textures and contrasts of light and dark, movement and stability. The different trees, the slow and splashing water, the glistening animals, the soft-textured hay bring energy and balance to the image. One senses a nature in which humanity is a fragile, yet persevering element in nature's larger "picture"...

**Fig. 2-11.
(Nellie Ladd)
Hauling hay
across the River.
c. 1905.**

44

**Fig. 2-12. (Nellie Ladd)
Leading the animals across
the Salmon River. c. 1905.**

Horses and mules are guided across the Salmon by Grover in this clas-sic Nellie Ladd photograph of water, energy, and the beauty of work in nature and nature at work. Nellie seemed fascinated by water, her photo-graphs capturing its movement, often in relation to animals and people. The power of the animals and the natural environment is evident in the scenes.

45

Fig. 2-13. (Nellie Ladd) Mules of the pack train steaming in the snow. c. 1900.

The Ladd pack train supplied merchandise and food for their own businesses and other clients and carried materials, and sometimes gold, out to towns to both the east and the west. The mules offered great scenes for Nellie Ladd to photograph, from her sons packing and leading the mules to the natural fog effect of steamy mule breath, body heat and movement in the snow. Nellie created a stunning photograph of the family pack train in Denny before loading or after unloading their packs in the snow. The photograph is alive with suspended movement, anticipation and energy. The foregrounding of the mules and the angle of the shot from below eye level adds to the sense of drama and animal energy. The effects are compounded by the number of mules, dark and white, photographed close together. The mules spent winters in Scott Valley.

46

Fig. 2-14. (Nellie Ladd) Grover and Willard Ladd guide the mule train across Mary Blaine Meadow (Pony Buttes backdrop). c. 1907.

The mule train on the trail was the subject of epic panorama photographs, rich in historical detail. One such photograph portrays Grover and Willard guiding the mules across a high mountain meadow as if in a Western film. In this photograph the boys cross Mary Blaine Meadow among the flowers, balsamroot flowers pictured in color in modern photographs on pages 155 and 156. Near this scene are a spring, a grassy campsite, and a rock on which Willard Ladd signed his name in 1915 *(see page 155)*. Another epic photograph on page 84 shows the mule train following a wooden flume that conducts water to the mines, probably along Slide Creek. Pack trains required (as they do still today) at least two guides on horseback, in case of falls, injury, snake bites or other emergencies. The Ladd pack train traveled southwest down New River and then to the west as far as Korbel and Arcata, and north to Forks of Salmon, Cecilville and Callahan.

47

Among Nellie Ladd's animal photographs was the popular favorite that Nellie titled "Tail-o-phone," picturing her husband Frank between two women who were communicating via the ears and the tail of a donkey. The telephone, which had arrived in Old Denny by 1912, was quite a phenomenon, and Nellie often spoke by telephone to her friends downriver, including Viola Dailey and Kate Irving, in the last decade of her life.

Fig. 2-15. (Nellie Ladd) "Tail-o-phone": Frank Ladd and two unidentified women with donkey. c. 1902. Self-titled.

Fig. 2-16. (Nellie Ladd)
Forks of Salmon. c. 1902.

Other subjects for Nellie's photography in the early 1900s were local towns and buildings, such as this photograph of Forks of Salmon, north of the New River area, in Siskiyou County *(see area sketch, page 3)*. Nellie captures the silence of a hot, dusty summer day in the small town seemingly uninhabited by human or animal. With a wide range of white to black, the photograph offers angles and perspective leading the eye to the central building and upper window. The haze of the sun against the forested hillside brings out the dark foregrounded porch shadow to the left and oak tree branches to the right, framing an empty white center.

49

The best-known family portrait is a gathering on the Ladd porch with Rose Ryan, a good friend of the boys, and Frank Patten *(right)*, who was working at the Gun Barrel Mine with Grover and Willard at about the same period. Balance and tranquillity reign in a comfortable domestic atmosphere. Nellie's chair seems to include her in the scene.

Fig. 2-17. (Nellie Ladd) The Ladd family, Rose Ryan and Frank Patten on the Ladd porch. c. 1905.

50

Nellie also took many portrait photographs of local individuals and couples. Often outside portraits were group shots, such as this photograph of the Pattersons taken on the Ladd porch. The porch, like the parlor, portrays a mood of grace and domesticity.

Stella Patterson appears here and in group photographs at the Boomer cookhouse. We know she lived with her husband Jim at what is now the Dailey Ranch, then in the Willow Creek area. From there she left for San Francisco on her own in about 1936. In her eighties, she moved back to northern California, to a mining claim in Happy Camp, where she lived alone and wrote a book about her experiences, titled *Dear Mad'm,* which received national acclaim.[4] *See page 119.*

Jim Patterson is shown in Nellie Ladd photographs with the community at the Boomer cookhouse *(see page 105)* and with the Ladd boys. Since the 1900 census *(see Appendix B)* lists him as a 17-year-old day laborer with his brother (on his father's farm or on his uncle Moses' homesteaded Oak Flat Farm, later to become the Dailey Ranch), we can date Fig. 2-18 at about 1907 from his appearance. Residents of Willow Creek today speak of young Jim's sawmill and mining enterprises in Hawkins Bar and mostly of his ranch on what is now Patterson Road in Willow Creek.[5]

Fig. 2-18. (Nellie Ladd) The Pattersons on the Ladd porch in Old Denny. c. 1907.

Fig. 2-19. (Nellie Ladd) Portrait of an unidentified couple and dog in the Ladd home.[6] c. 1910.

Nellie Ladd's interior artificial lighting photographs reflect balance and texture. The play of contrasting black and white complements the masculine and feminine subjects, while greeting cards and a dog on the bed add human and animal interest. The flags in the Ladd home that appear in many photographs are at once decor, representations of civic duty and patriotism, and a reminder that mountain folk were conscious of national and also international events. The local newspapers covered the War of 1898. The Ladd boys registered for the draft and Willard enlisted in the Army in World War I, serving as private in Co. A, 319 Engineers. (For some reason, Grover did not.) National magazines found in Denny included photographs of the 1900 Paris Exhibition and the National Women's Congress in Iowa.

52

Seemingly a companion piece of Fig. 2-19, the previous photograph, the portrait of Mr. and Mrs. Hotchkiss repeats the use and balance of black and white dress, the play of texture, and the warm shine of the polished wooden arm on Nellie's rocking chair. Another photograph including Mr. and Mrs. Hotchkiss is the cookhouse group portrait at the Mountain Boomer Mine *(see page 105).*

Both husband and wife were mine owners. Emma J. Hotchkiss located the Kismet Mine, and M. S. Hotchkiss claimed the Pearl Mine, both on June 8, 1898. Several others claimed mines that day, including Frank Ladd, and probably all the miners traveled to Weaverville together to record their claims.

Fig. 2-20. (Nellie Ladd) Portrait of Mr. and Mrs. Hotchkiss in the Ladd home. c. 1910.

53

The human figure takes second place to the mining environment in Nellie Ladd photographs beginning in about 1913, the year the Tener Mine and community at Robber's Roost were established. Nellie photographed the monitors or "giants" that shot out water to blast apart hillside and riverbed earth and gravel to reveal quartz and gold. In this striking photograph, the solitary dark figure observes, as we do, the water stream that sprays out, rushing by the wooden sluice behind it. The play of sunlight and shadow adds complexity to the contrast of vivid black human figure and earth against the whiteness of sprayed water and foreground patches of snow. Water (power) was abundant during the spring run-off.

Fig. 2-21. (Nellie Ladd) A monitor, a man and a sluice, probably on Slide Creek. c. 1915.

Nellie took several wintry photographs of Robber's Roost, where the Tener Mine miners lived from about 1913 or 1915 to 1918. The sharp contrast in Fig. 2-22 between blackened wet buildings and brilliant white snow is softened by shadow and snowy trees. The three distant figures give the photograph depth and human context. This photograph may have been taken at the same time period as the cover photograph that Nellie titled, "Coming Down." See a "before and after" comparison of Fig. 2-22 and the same scene in a recent photograph on page 153. For photographs of the Tener Mine operations, see pages 80, 81, 83, and 85.

Fig. 2-22. (Nellie Ladd) Robber's Roost in the snow. c. 1915.

From the rough to the romantic, Nellie captured the images of the historical events taking place in her mining community and also took time to smell the roses--and to photograph the hollyhocks. She took two negative photographs of the same garden scene, changing the direction of the woman's gaze and including, or not, the edge of a building to the right. In both shots the woman down the path is in focus, while the foregrounded plants to the left are not. The woman's dress and hat *(compare to those of Rose Ryan, page 50)* confirm the romantic mood of the flower-lined path. The building angles frame the scene and add an interesting texture, while the shadows below the shingles and the path itself direct the observer's gaze to the central figure.

The scene is most likely just north of the Larcine Hotel, whose small accessory structure *(see page 97, far left)* has the same shingle construction. The open woods are similar. The most striking clue tying the photographs together was a small plant noted by researchers in Marysville in 2001, and then, in 2002, its blooms 7 to 8 feet high of white double hollyhocks, just north of the site of the Larcine Hotel, not long after the 1999 forest fire *(see page 154)*. Hollyhocks also grace the Larcine fireplace photographs on pages 20 and 32.

Fig. 2-23. (Nellie Ladd) "Hollyhock Walk": Woman in the hollyhocks. c. 1905. Self-titled.

Nellie Ladd's photography ranged from the historical to the poetic, from the humorous to the sublime. It was historically invaluable, both from the standpoint of local mining history and from the viewpoint of the development of early amateur photography. Both her photographs and her life juxtaposed the unique and the universal, leaving a legacy that scholarly art critics may tend

Fig. 2-24. (Nellie Ladd) Willard on the porch. c. 1905.

to call, in fact, "more historical than artistic," but which her admirers see as an important artistic collection revealing an eye for beauty and composition. Local history has indeed taken concrete shape in her images, which then guide researchers in their studies of upper New River mine and town sites. But her art, as well, her sense of the play of wood, textures, angles, snow, water, light and shadow, flowing drapery and forms of a favorite chair or dress, put the stories it tells on a universal artistic plane where the photograph makes the history of daily life "something to remember" as a work of art.

NOTES

CHAPTER II

1. Gay Holland, obituary: "Grover Ladd, Pioneer of New River Area, Succombs," *Trinity Journal,* January, 1973.

2. Peter Palmquist lecture at opening of the photo exhibit "Nellie Ladd: Woman Photographer Among the Mules, Miners and Merchants," hosted by U. S. Forest Service archeological technician Gay Holland Berrien, at the Morris Graves Museum of Art, Eureka, CA, June 27, 2000.

3. *Sears, Roebuck and Co., Inc. Consumers Guide, Fall 1900,* miniature reproduction (Northfield, Illinois: DBI Books, 1970), pp. 186-187.

4. Stella Walthall Patterson, *Dear Mad'm* (Happy Camp, CA: Naturegraph Publishers, 1982; reprint 2002 with photograph of the author). See more about Stella Patterson in Margaret Wooden, "History of the Pat- terson Ranch on Patterson Road," *Footprints in the Sands of Time* (news- letter of the Willow Creek-China Flat Museum in Willow Creek, CA): Winter 2003, 1-4.

5. Jim Patterson is shown in the group photograph on page 105. Infor- mation is from Gay Berrien and local historians Margaret Wooden and Max Rowley, who first met both Stella and Jim Patterson in 1936. Wooden and Rowley knew the story of the Pattersons from the per- spective of their Trinity River associations and marriage. The marriage did not last, however; Stella moved away to San Francisco, while Jim stayed in Willow Creek on his ranch. For more information on Jim (B.) Patterson, see note 4: Margaret Wooden, "History of the Patterson Ranch on Patterson Road," 2003.

6. See also page 63, Fig. 3-3, where the same man stands in front of a double mine adit with a friend.

There are bonanzas in the air--New River bonanzas. Prospective millionaires stand on every street corner of Eureka, and "specimens" may be found on every counter. The excitement is growing day by day. It is in the air. Like the politi- cal excitement of last Fall, the mining excitement of to-day permeates all classes and fires the imagi- nation, if not the passions, of old and young.

--Eureka *Times-Telephone,* Jan. 17, 1885

CHAPTER III

The Mines of New River

Stephen Sherwood (1811-1894)
Photograph courtesy of Grant Davis.

It is but recently that vein mining has been prosecuted in this locality. The (New River) district was discovered and brought into notice by Mr. Stephen Sherwood, a '49er frontiersman and inveterate prospector, who, like the Wandering Jew, drifted from place to place in search of new discoveries, fresher fields and fairer flowers. He discovered Meadow Valley, Pioche and many other valuable districts. While in the vicinity of Shasta this mineral belt attracted his attention. He followed it until he camped in what is known as the New River District, exclaiming, "Eureka."

--Trinity Journal, Jan. 10, 1885

A legend was born, with Stephen Sherwood as its hero. News of the gold rush picked up from local newspapers had been taken up by the San Francisco *Evening Post* on Jan. 2, 1885. Then the *Trinity Journal* reprinted it on Jan. 10 (above). The *Mining and Scientific Press* copied the same story Jan. 24, adding a geological description of the mining district on upper New River, a tributary of the Trinity River:

The ledges run at right angles with the vein...for 60 miles more or less. This belt is composed of slates (serpentines and allied metamorphic rocks) with intrusive dykes of diorite (greenstone trap), syenite and porphyry. The veins are, as a rule, small, varying from a few inches to several feet, the gangue, ferruginous quartz, carrying free gold--the line of decomposition probably extending to a considerable depth. The altitude being about 4,000 feet, the snows of the winter soon melt and run off. The side-hill is densely covered with timber--fir, pine and oak. The branches of the streams all carry running water--crystal springs of icy coldness are often seen. Water for motive power is obtainable in the creeks in near proximity to the mines.[1]

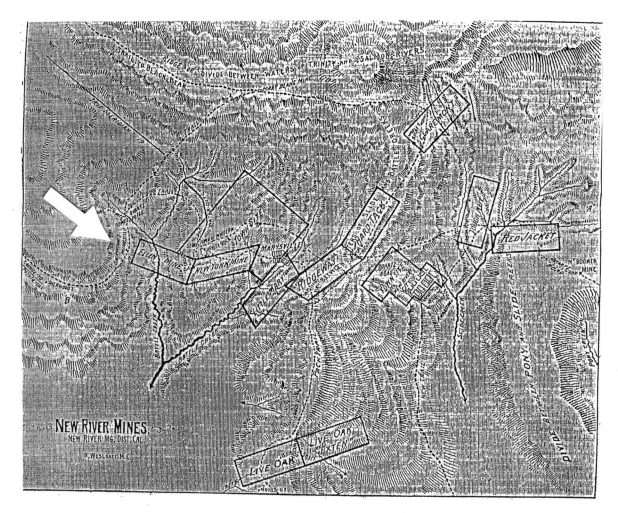

The *Mining and Scientific Press* article included a map of many of the mines and the three town sites of White Rock, Marysville and New River City at the beginning of 1885.[2] "Sherwood's mines," which included the **Gold King**, the **Sherwood**, the **Climax**, the **Carry**, and the **Pony**, are west of White Rock *(see arrow)*. The fork of Battle Creek below the Sherwood mines became known as Sherwood Creek.

Fig. 3-1. Map of New River Mines, New River Mining District, California, by N. Wescoatt, Mining Engineer. Arrow marks Sherwood mines.

1882 The *Trinity Journal* records both Sherwood's cry of "Eureka" and the Clement/Clemens discovery ("his partner, F.J. Ladd, will also be here shortly") Sept. 17-30, 1882, the two discoveries setting off the upper New River district mining boom.[3] The less trustworthy Trinity County index shows Sherwood's five mines recorded in August, 1883, and Ladd and Clement's **Mountain Boomer** in December, 1882. Other miners staking upper New River hardrock claims in 1882 included Hely and Kerby, Boyle, Boles, Corsen, Hodges, Huff, Lawton and Mills. Hely is listed as recording the first hardrock ledge, the **Confidence**, on Eagle Creek, followed by the **Ridgeway**.[4]

60

It is in 1882 that Frank Ladd's name first appears in the county records. His friend Oliver Clement or Clemens included Ladd's name when he claimed Slide Creek water rights, a mill site, the **Mountain Boomer** and the **Hard Tack** mines. With Clement and John Clifford Frank Ladd located the **Hunter** and the **Hoo-che-noo** in 1883.[5] The Mountain Boomer Mine was a mile from Old Denny across tributaries of Slide Creek. It became the most successful mine in the district, extracting an estimated $350,000 worth of gold by 1901.[6] The Boomer was part of a group of three mines, with the **Tough Nut** (1883) and the **Red Jacket** (1885).[7]

From the **Excelsior** stamp mill on the outskirts of Old Denny, miners took the "Excelsior Road" southeast around the steep canyon and across one branch of Slide Creek to the Tough Nut, then across another branch of Slide Creek to the hill-side with the Boomer cookhouse above and the Ladd home and the mill below. Across the mill stream, the road led to many mine adits, the Lewises' boarding house, cabins and other mines, such as the **Hidden Treasure**.

Fig. 3-2. (Nellie Ladd) Up to the mines: Pack train heading up the Excelsior Road toward the Boomer cookhouse. c. 1903.

1883   Stephen Sherwood claimed his five mines. Frank Ladd and Oliver Clement recorded the **Hoo-che-noo** and the **Hunter** mines, and T. J. Baker claimed the **Tough Nut**. Other new mines recorded in 1883 (according to the county index) included the **Leora**, the **Mary Blaine**, the **White Elephant**, and the **Ellen**.[8]

1884   The number of mine locations, relocations, mill sites, water claims and "agreements" exploded in 1884. Frank Ladd and Oliver Clement claimed water on New River, a mill site, and a Hard Tack relocation. The new mines of 1884,[9] as listed in the Trinity County index, included:

the **Eureka**,	the **Rocky Point**,	the **May** or **Mary Bell**,
the **Nevada**,	the **High Tone**,	the **New York** and the **Gilt Edge**,
the **Mary Blaine no. 2**,	the **Big Chief**,	the **Huntington**,
the **Stella**,	the **Claremont**,	the **Trinity King**,
the **Oro Fino**,	the **Inez May**,	the **Mountain Chief**,
the **Thunder Bolt**,	the **Tom Tom**,	the **Occident**, the **Orient**,
the **North Star**,	the **Nevada**,	and the **Argonaut**.

1885   The county records list the location by Frank Ladd, John Clifford, & Oliver Clement of both the Mountain Boomer and the **Red Jacket** mines in 1885. The Boomer notation may have referred to a re-purchase, when Ladd and Clement bought it at auction for $7,650 after their partnership with Clifford was dissolved.[10]

Frank Ladd and a Mr. Le Vafor (Levasseur?) were also awarded an "unacknowledged" deed by H. S. Soule *et al* (probably H. A. Libby and Christopher Luther) later that year. Mines and claims changed hands frequently, according to individual fortunes.

The names of other new mines in 1885 were the stuff of so many dreams: [11]

the **Hidden Treasure**	the **Bald Eagle**	the **Eastern Star**	the **Pony Creek Boomer**
the **Big Blue**	the **Rosina**	the **McCracken**	the **Luther**
the **D. R. Jones**	the **Cape Horn**	the **Celeena**	the **Pierce**
the **George L. Fisher**	the **Live Oak**	the **Key Stone**	the **Rocky Rim**
the **Holy Terror**	the **Argo**	the **Mustang**	and the **Ajax**.
the **St. Elmo**	the **Hummingbird**		

Hardrock mine adits

Fig. 3-3. (Nellie Ladd) Two miners and two adits. c. 1900.

A classic mining photograph taken by Nellie Ladd records the double adits, or mine entrances, of a hardrock mine.[12] It gives the flavor, the excitement, and the sense of the enormous effort involved in the digging of the horizontal passage into the hillside following a vein of gold. Some adits were cut through solid rock, while others, in fractured rock, were easier to dig and less safe to work. Explosives, toxic fumes, floods, snakes and other animals offered their own challenges to the miners. One man in this photograph seems to have a bandaged hand. The other *(right)* also appears in Fig. 2-19, page 52.

Hardrock miners lived a rugged life. First they traveled and climbed between forty and a hundred miles of trails from the closest population hub to reach the upper New River mines. Sometimes they and their pack animals fell off the steep trails into the canyons. Sometimes the miners suffered broken bones, crushed by boulders, or got sick and died alone. If they remained healthy enough, they climbed steep hillsides for months at a time searching for signs of gold: white quartz rock outcroppings or gold flakes in creek beds. After traveling back down to Weaverville to record a claim, they returned to the back-breaking work of digging mine passages, making lumber to shore them up, and digging long ditches across the hillsides to carry water from creeks and springs upstream down to their mine sites. All such work had to be maintained regularly. The miners worked in temperatures as high as 110 degrees in the summer and as low as zero in the winter, with blizzards in the coldest periods and avalanches as the snow became less stable during warming periods. Creek beds offering telltale signs of gold also harbored snakes, bears, and mountain lions. A miner breaking a leg or getting pneumonia might well die, even when not threatened by predators. And yet the miners continued to come to realize their dreams.

Inside the dark mines their work continued, with pick axes soon dulled by the granite and, hopefully, the quartz. Shovels broke and were abandoned. Successful miners could order ore cars and rails to be hauled in to the district. But many just loaded their mules with the ore, generally with about 300 pounds per mule, but sometimes with up to 400 pounds. Local blacksmiths were engaged to make candle holders from iron. These were pounded into cracks in the mine walls or mine timbers to hold candles that offered welcome but feeble light to those digging their way toward gold. The Pelton wheel first arrived in 1902 to provide electricity from water power, then electric lines came to the mines in 1912.

Nellie's photograph of Jack Martin and fellow miner inside a mine *(Fig. 3-4, page 65)* shows rare sunbeams filtering into the darkness of an adit near its entrance. Miners often worked through the winter, since temperatures inside the mines were moderate. Grover and Willard Ladd, along with their friend Frank Patten, kept a diary of their routine in January and February of 1907 while "digging a tunnel," as they wrote, at the **Gun Barrel Mine**.[13] See photos of modern researchers exploring the Meckel Crosscut adit at the Boomer on pages 150 and 163.

Fig. 3-4 (Nellie Ladd) Rare sunbeams find Jack Martin and unknown man (right) **inside a mine adit. c. 1900.**

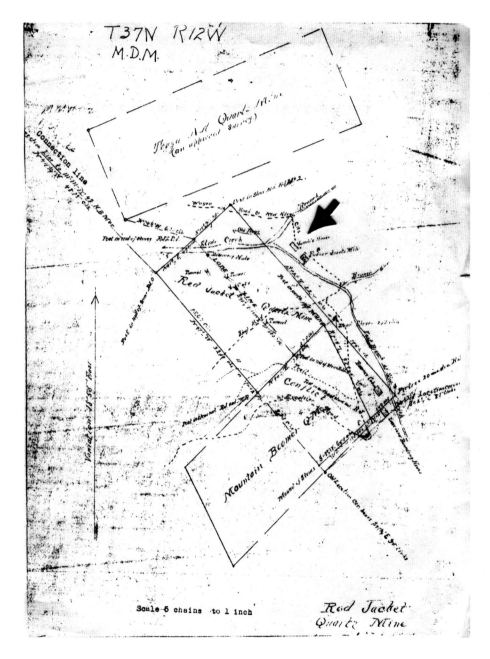

Scale 5 chains to 1 inch

Red Jacket
Quartz Mine

The Mountain Boomer

A remarkable survey map of the Mountain Boomer, the Red Jacket and the Tough Nut mines shows the tributaries of Slide Creek that powered machinery of the Mountain Boomer Mine. The black arrow indicates where the Ladds lived, on a steep slope between two rushing streams, just downhill of the "Excelsior Road" that ran from the Old Denny area to the mines beyond. Uphill from the Ladd house, about at the point of the arrow, the Boomer cookhouse was built in 1902. The road continues past the stamp mill--"Boomer quatrz mill" on the map--across a stream to the mine adits. The "lode line," which is the NW-SE center line of the Red Jacket claim, marks the probable location of the vein of gold-bearing quartz, and the survey shows many "tunnels" or mine adits along this line. John Lewis was killed outside his boarding house, shown near the SE corner of the Boomer claim, hit by an avalanche in the same 1890 storm that hit the Ladd home and almost killed Frank Ladd.

The 2002 and 2003 archeological expeditions used this survey to begin work on a Boomer Mine area site record.

Fig. 3-5. 1880s survey of the Mountain Boomer, Red Jacket and Tough Nut mines.

Nellie photographed many operations at the **Mountain Boomer Mine**. The "mill stream," as noted on the back of this photograph from a glass plate, provided water for the flume and ditch built in 1892. The *Trinity Journal* reported late in 1891:

> Clement and Ladd of the Boomer mine are constructing a ditch, by which they expect to convey water around a point called the Boomer hill to the mine, for the purpose of hydraulicking several thousand tons of surface dirt, considered very rich in mineral.[14]

Water was critical for mining operations, and miners awaited its arrival each winter with great anticipation. In addition to several mill streams, a more dependable water and power source for the Mountain Boomer was the Boomer pond and its spring *(see page 162)*, located about a mile uphill to the east, just below the Salmon divide. A large pipe ran from the pond down to the mine, where small diameter pipes split to furnish water power to different parts of the operation. The pipe to the cookhouse was said to have run a Pelton wheel under the kitchen sink, providing electricity to the elegant steep-sloped building. Today only the pipe coming down the hill and a trough for the water runoff remain.

Fig. 3-6. (Nellie Ladd) Mill stream and flume at the Boomer Mine. c. 1896.
Original photograph, from glass plate.

The **Mountain Boomer Mine** was not only near Slide Creek but was itself situated on slide-prone ground, which complicated mining operations, according to *Mining and Scientific Press* in early 1885.[15] After the Ladds left Old Denny and the Boomer in 1921, the mine was worked sporadically by Frederick C. Meckel until the 1940s.[16]

Nellie's glass plate photograph shows the tramway from one of the adits, used to transport ore to the stamp mill built after early operations with the arrastra and a water wheel.[17] Piles of lumber at the lower left recall two big building ventures at the Boomer. First, in 1892, Frank invested in a large amount of lumber to build a flume to the mine *(see Fig. 3-6, page 67)*. In 1902, he had the cookhouse built. Here the sawmill may be producing the lumber for the cookhouse.

Fig. 3-7. (Nellie Ladd) The Mountain Boomer Mine buildings, lumber, mine adit, flume and tramways. c. 1902. Glass slide.

A very different Nellie Ladd photograph portrays the same tramway system with construction in progress. The three-stamp mill had already been in existence since 1891, crushing and separating the ore; perhaps this was new housing for the old mill. Three brave men pose on the upper reaches of the roof frame. Stacks of roof shingles lie ready for the construction. The camera seems suspended in mid air, though the previous photograph suggests a large debris pile may have given the photographer access to this scene. The sky behind surrounds the men, filling a full third of the photograph. The trees point gracefully upward, as do the men atop their A-line vertical construction. Other elements of the scene, including beams and ladders, give an impression of upward movement. The man standing on the trestle may be Bert Brackett.

The forest backdrop in this photograph shows large trees, while other mine photographs picture substantial deforestation. See Nellie Ladd photograph Fig. 5-2, page 127, and a modern view of the same scene, Fig. 6-43, page 153, indicating reforestation of the Old Denny area.

Fig. 3-8. (Nellie Ladd) The Boomer tramway trestle leads to the mill housing under construction. c. 1903.

Water power for the **Boomer** arrastra was supplied by a huge 33-foot overshot water wheel. Weight of water in the three-foot deep buckets in the wheel turned it to run a 16-foot pulley, which turned the arrastra.[18]

A Nellie Ladd water wheel photograph, which has since then disappeared from the main collection, was featured in Florence Morris's article, "A Tale of Three Cities" in the Trinity County Historical Society yearbook, *Trinity 1970*. In this photograph, copied from the yearbook, man is subordinated to the huge equipment of mining operations. A man and perhaps a boy in front of him observe the water wheel from lower center of the photograph, seemingly caught between two enormous pieces of machinery. Yet man and boy seem comfortable in their place among the machines, an optimism reflected as well in the sunlight streaming through the planks that make up the walls of the mill. Morris tells us the wheel was made of whip-sawed sugar pine.[19]

Fig. 3-9. (Nellie Ladd) 33-foot overshot wheel at the Mountain Boomer. c. 1902.
Courtesy of the Trinity Co. Historical Society.

Fig. 3-10. (Nellie Ladd) Frank Patten (left),
Willard Ladd (center) **and unknown man
under the Gun Barrel Mine arrastra. c. 1906.**

The arrastra built by Frank Ladd for the **Boomer** in 1883 probably looked something like the one built much later by the Ladds, Frank Patten and others for the **Gun Barrel Mine**, pictured above.[20] After the day's work, sometimes the arrastra continued during the night as well. Pulled by cables, its drag stones crushed ore and released the gold, which remained on the bottom of the arrastra tub until it was cleaned out.[21]

71

Fig. 3-11. (Nellie Ladd) Workers inside the the Boomer Mine stamp mill. c. 1910.

Workers appear to control the operation of pulley, stamps, ramps, and ladders in the stamp mill pictured in one of Nellie's most successful photographs, in terms of both art and history. It pictures the three-stamp mill that replaced the arrastra operation at the **Boomer Mine**. The stamps are visible in the upper center of the photograph. The dark backdrop is lit by sunlight from above, and by light which comes from behind the camera from another outside opening. The camera captures a full range of shades from white to black and textures of rough boot soles, ruddy complexions, and rough-cut timbers.

Fig. 3-12. (Nellie Ladd) The Boomer stamp mill, workers, lumber from the sawmill (out of the picture to the left) **and tramway. c. 1902.**

The work of the **Mountain Boomer** sawmill impressed Nellie Ladd, the photographer, with its large production of lumber and its busy crew. In this photograph at least four men work among the boards between the sawmill and the stamp mill. The three stamps are visible in the stamp mill, the second building from the right, perhaps with the older mill housing. The tramway from the right brings the ore to be crushed.

The human side of the mines is portrayed in this Nellie Ladd photograph of "Little Byerlie," the Byers' son, who also had his picture taken with a bear after a bear hunt. In this portrait, taken at the **Mountain Boomer** Mine, the boy holds a gold pan. His squatting position looks like that of a faint figure in Fig. 3-9, page 70, just in front of the man next to the giant water wheel. Here, however, Little Byerlie is foregrounded and centered, apparently ready for a future in mining.

Fig. 3-13. (Nellie Ladd) Little Byerlie with a gold pan at the Mountain Boomer Mine. c. 1904.

Wall construction in this photograph is similar to that of the now-fallen interior walls of the Boomer cookhouse, observed in summer 2003 *(see page 149)*.

The **Boomer** cookhouse, built in 1902, was an impressive building with an equally impressive view. Nellie photographed it from above and below *(see pages 11, 61, 149)* and also took this photograph of a man aiming his rifle from the cookhouse vantage point. The composition of the photo is striking, with many of the scene's elements guiding the eye to the center: clothesline, fallen timber, roof line, construction lumber and pile of roof shingles. Meanwhile the rifle itself points out of the photograph. For the modern viewer, the photograph has a Chaplinesque quality. Notice the practical function of the stump behind the man in the photograph.

Though the mining boom lasted only from about 1883 to 1894, the Mountain Boomer continued to be successful and sporadically employed a large number of workers well into the 20th century.

Fig. 3-14. (Nellie Ladd) Zeroing in a rifle at the Boomer cookhouse. c. 1905.

75

The Tough Nut

The **Tough Nut**, just across Slide Creek from the **Boomer**, was located in 1883 by T. J. Baker. According to the *Mining and Scientific Press* in 1885, it had a ledge 16 inches wide, with an adit running level along the vein for 50 feet.[22] It produced nearly 600 ounces of gold, largely for Oliver Clement, Frank Ladd and later Grover and Willard, who also owned it.[23] This mine was patented and is still private property in the middle of the Trinity Alps Wilderness. It was the home of Smokey Bergstrom and his family in the 1970s. Bergstrom, who still lives in (new) Denny, describes the mine operations on the hillside: 40-foot drifts, or horizontal passages following the vein of gold, were dug into the mountainside, but after awhile each would flood from seepage, and a new drift would be dug until it, too, flooded out. Bergstrom finally found that the elusive vein of gold came up to the surface in the meadow of his property.[24]

The Hunter

The **Hunter** occupied 100 acres about a half-mile north of Old Denny and was connected by road to the Ridgeway stamp mill to the south and the Sherwood mines to the north. Frank Ladd and Oliver Clement located the Hunter in 1883, working it along with the **Boomer**, the **Hard Tack**, and the **Tough Nut.** The Hunter produced silver, as well as gold; from 1892 to 1905, 198 ounces of gold and 15 ounces of silver.[25] The *Trinity Journal* reported that Nellie and Celina Larcine (who was a prospector herself) spent the day with Mrs. Charles Jacobs at the Hunter Mine in September of 1911.[26] The 2001 archeological expedition to the site found a six-foot high pile of white quartz ore at a caved-in adit of the mine, left unprocessed by miners, the last of whom was Andy Jacobsen, who died there in 1941.

The Hard Tack

THe **Hard Tack**, adjacent to the **Hunter**, was claimed by Ladd and Clement in 1882. The Hard Tack was both earlier and more successful over the long haul than its neighbor, producing 873 ounces of gold.[27] Its vein, according to *Mining and Scientific Press*, was 15 inches wide. Its shaft ran 62 feet deep, and its drifts ran 30 feet.[28]

The Sherwood

The metal production of the **Sherwood Mine** (located in 1882) from 1889 to 1901 was 3,652 ounces of gold and 159 ounces of silver. The mine operated early on with a two-stamp mill, and later its ore was transported by road to the Ridgeway mill.[29]

The Cinnabar

The **Cinnabar** Mine, also known at different times as the **Esther** or the **Blue Jay Nos. 1** and **2**,[30] near Mary Blaine Meadow, mined the red cinnabar ore, producing from it quicksilver, or mercury. The mine was established by Peter Larcine and later run by Charles Hahn. In 1941 the *California Journal of Mines and Geology* stated, "New River District contains several quicksilver prospects, and seven or eight flasks of quicksilver have been produced in recent years by Charles Hahn, who used a retort."[31] Today the mercury retort still stands at the mine site, in crimson paintbrush wildflowers. *(See page 157.)*

The Ridgeway

The **Ridgeway Mine,** located downhill from Marysville, had the biggest stamp mill in the district, with ten half-ton stamps and one-ton batteries or mortars. It took six weeks to haul two of these mortars from Etna south to Helena on the Trinity River, up the North Fork of the Trinity to Rattlesnake and Grizzly creeks, and finally over the divide and down to the mine.[32]

Fig. 3-15. (Nellie Ladd) The Ridgeway Mine. c. 1910. Courtesy of Dick Holland.

The **Ridgeway** was discovered by G. V. Hely in 1882.[33] By 1885 it was considered to be the "best mine so far in the district,"[34] "fabulously rich."[35] Its mill ran on steam from boilers still visible today alongside the ten stamps exposed when the mill burned down in 1999. An older mill was destroyed, like the Ladd home, by an avalanche in 1890. At the lower right of the photograph is the bottom of an enormous pile of rock debris from the 900-foot tunnel into the hillside that failed to produce the expected gold.[36] The Ridgeway mill was connected by a 5000-foot tramway to mines uphill and, by road, north to the **Hunter,** the **Ellen,** and the **Sherwood** mines.

Bob's Farm Mine ?[37]

Up Rattlesnake Creek from the North Fork of the Trinity was Bob's Farm Mine. Nellie Ladd knew and photographed the Byers, who worked on the Mountain Boomer Mine and were part owners in Bob's Farm Mine, where Nellie may have accompanied them and taken this photograph, Fig. 3-16, and the following one, Fig. 3-17. At this time the Mountain Boomer was also part of the Bob's Farm Company.[38] Lines, textures, and angles make this a particularly artistic study.

Fig. 3-16. (Nellie Ladd)
Bob's Farm Mine?
c. 1904.
Glass plate.

Nellie seems to have taken an experimental photograph of what may be the ore chute and buildings of **Bob's Farm Mine**, given the terrain and descriptions of the mine. The photograph's title "Wm M-- Fallen tree by B. F. M." seems to corroborate the hypothesis.[39]

Like Fig. 3-16, this photograph accentuates artistic elements of the mine site rather than recording it for history.

Fig. 3-17. (Nellie Ladd) Ore chute, possibly at Bob's Farm Mine.
Photograph is self-titled: **"Wm M-- Fallen tree by B.F. M."**[40]
c. 1904.

79

Tener Mine

Fig. 3-18. (Nellie Ladd)
Three men at the head
of a sluice. c. 1915.

The **Tener Mine** was not a hardrock mine but a placer operation beginning on Slide Creek near the mouth of Emigrant Creek. Nellie photographed the upper end of the sluice, where miners helped funnel gold and gravel, loosened from the riverbank by the monitor's water blast, into the wooden sluice, in the bottom of which blocks of wood or similar obstructions would cause the gold to settle, while the other materials continued down the sluice and out the other end. In this photograph, background misty forest and foaming white water lead downstream and left, to a darkening, more sharply focused rocky foreground with three men at work on the sluice approach.

Fig. 3-19. (Nellie Ladd) "Giant" hydraulicking above the sluice on Slide Creek. c. 1915.

The wide expanse of the Slide Creek riverbed and its banks near Robber's Roost held deposits of gold that giants blasted from the earth. Water from flumes and ditches high above the monitors, held in a pond and released into pipes, rushed down to power these monitors. The sluice pictured in this photograph had a division point just above the lower right of the scene, so the sluice could go to two different sides of the flat.

In the Sierra Nevada range to the southeast, hydraulic mining operations were required to be licensed by the California Debris Commission, established in 1893, in order to create tailings storage dams and protect river habitat. There were no such controls on the Trinity River or its tributaries.[41]

Nellie Ladd captured the epic quality of the mountain mining enterprise in her photograph of Grover and Willard guiding the mules of the Ladd pack train along a flume built to supply water to the "giants" and other mining operations. Howard May notes that every foot of rise above the "giant" provided it with 0.443 psi of water pressure.[42]

Fig. 3-20. (Nellie Ladd) Grover and Willard Ladd with the pack train, following the flume above Slide Creek. c. 1915.

**Fig. 3-21. (Nellie Ladd)
Water exits the sluice,
possibly into Slide Creek.
c. 1915.**

At the end of the sluice, the diverted water and gravel re-entered the riverbed in a rush, leaving a good proportion of its gold behind blocks of wood on the bottom of the box. In this photograph the man rests on the structure, as if to admire the miners' handiwork and successful exploitation of the power of the environment. The presence of a woman, dressed in white and holding a dog, defies the harsh environment and celebrates the mining process.

83

Grover Ladd's pack train hauled in pipe and other supplies for this surface operation. As late as 1971 Grover told Gay Holland (Berrien) of his hauls to the **Tener Mine** from Callahan, to the northeast: 1,700 feet of mining pipe ranging in diameter from 11" to 18," parts for a sawmill and a 48" Pelton wheel to supply water power for the mill, "an American Mill No. 1, equipped with a 48-inch saw."[43] Pipe similar to the sections in this photograph still lie at the sites of the Mountain Boomer and the Red Jacket mines, and also the Sherwood.

Fig. 3-22. (Nellie Ladd) Hauling in the pipe. c. 1906.

The Tener Mine sawmill cut the lumber for the long flume, creating the high water pressure necessary to break up rock and gravel and separate out the gold. Grover remembered that ten to twelve men ran this placer operation in two shifts and found a good amount of gold, but, he said, "They didn't clean it up very well."[44] Given the rough terrain, gold ofen slipped in between rocks and did not reach the sluice; later miners found gold where the early hydraulic miners had worked with their giants. A heavy piece of placer mining equipment, probably part of a pump, can still be seen downstream near the mouth of Virgin Creek.

Fig. 3-23. (Nellie Ladd) Mr. Cowen (center) **and friends tugging the giant to a new location. c. 1915.**

The **Tener Mine** operation owned two big monitors--
"giants"-- that blasted the earth, using the power of the water under pressure to separate gold from the debris.
The major work at the Tener took place from 1915 to 1918.[45] In this sharply-focused action photograph, J. A.
"Gus" Cowen and others haul one of the giants to a new position on Slide Creek. The men tug their equipment
along, smiling for the photographer, in a setting of rock and delicate leaf patterns. *(See Mrs. Cowen, page 115.)*

Meanwhile, in Siskiyou County...

The Gun Barrel

Frank, Grover and Willard Ladd, Frank Patten and others worked the **Gun Barrel Mine**, not far over the Salmon River divide north of Mary Blaine Peak. They used the Black Bear Post Office for their correspondence home. In 1906 Frank Patten built a trail to the mine, a trail that the Ladds later continued to Plummer Creek.[46]

Historian Margaret Wooden explains that this Nellie Ladd photograph at the Gun Barrel Mine pictures a whipsaw pit. Once a log was rolled onto the platform, the upper man pulled the saw up and the pit man pulled it down. The canvas under the platform was nailed up to keep most of the sawdust off the pit man.[47] A patient pup balances the scene in shape, texture, shade of black, and qualities of passivity and domesticity. His position contrasts the uprightness of trees and builders and the energetic sense of purpose and control of the miners.

Fig. 3-24. (Nellie Ladd) Whipsaw pit at the Gun Barrel Mine. c. 1906-1907.

**Fig. 3-25.
(Nellie Ladd)
Top view of
the Gun Barrel
arrastra with
Frank Patten.
c. 1906.**

Both the miner-builders and the photographer were proud of the new arrastra, its 24-foot span, its regular angles and curves making its place in the wilderness. The positioning of the eye of the viewer above the arrastra, level with Frank Patten and another worker in a tree to the far right, accentuates the people involved in the project, as they stand overlooking their creation. Notice what looks like a birdhouse just below the arrastra, to the left of the tree. The other photograph of this arrastra, on page 71, emphasizes construction over builders.

The Gun Barrel arrastra included a more sophisticated ore tub from which the crushed rock exited through discharge holes onto a table extending from it. Three foot square mercury plates on the table separated the gold from the other elements of the ore. Florence Morris notes that these "quicksilver plates" cost as much as $45 each, a substantial investment at the time.[48]

The photograph of the ore discharge system is an image of accomplishment and confidence. The proud builders stand above the photographer and the dark earth below. All around them, the fruits of their labor shine in the light, the arrastra wheel above almost celestial in appearance. The giant trees to the far right and left frame both work and workers and confirm the achievement.

Compare this ore chute to the one pictured on page 79, Fig. 3-17, which may be at Bob's Farm Mine.

Fig. 3-26. (Nellie Ladd) The Gun Barrel Mine arrastra ore discharge system. c. 1907.

Many years before Robber's Roost housed miners of the Tener Mine, these buildings were constructed for the **Gun Barrel Mine** workers. This Nellie Ladd photograph, in contrast with the whipsaw pit, arrastra and ore discharge photographs, is rather bucolic. The

Fig. 3-27. (Nellie Ladd) The buildings at the Gun Barrel Mine. c. 1908.

sun-dappled forest seems to hold the tiny community in its branches and shade, a pleasant place to work and live, at least in the summer. When the boys wrote postcards home to their mother from the Gun Barrel, they wrote affectionately of girlfriends, family and others, in a lighthearted spirit. It was here, though, that Frank Patten and the boys spent long, hard winter days and months digging the mine tunnel in early 1907.

NOTES
CHAPTER III

1. Article and map, *Mining & Scientific Press,* Jan. 24, 1885, p. 53.

2. See note 1 above.

3. The *Trinity Journal* first reported the find Sept. 30, 1882 (from New River, Sept. 17, 1882): "F. M. Kerby and Mr. Sherwood found some very rich croppings last June and with very little trouble discovered the ledge from which they came...still another was found by a man--O. Clement..."; *Trinity Journal,* Dec. 9, 1882.

4. Mining claims registered at the Trinity County courthouse were researched by Gay Holland Berrien, in Trinity County indexes from 1871 to 1899. She notes that in some years the county registrar omitted the mining district from each entry, so Berrien only copied those she thought were from New River, by recognizing either the claim or the claimant names. Thus the list she developed is not complete. There are also some index errors in the names and dates of the mines. The claim information for the years 1882 to 1885 comes mostly from the county index data. Fewer mines were located after 1885.

In 1882 Hely located the **Ridgeway**, according to the county index and the *Trinity Journal,* Jan. 10, 1885:

> "In 1882 G. V. Healey, striking out from the settlement of Francis, located at the forks of New River, went up the stream some twenty miles, and following up Eagle Creek to its source, located the **Confidence Mine**. Crossing the divide to Slide Creek he discovered and located the **Ridgeway,** which has proven to be the best mine so far in the district."

Other new mines, left nameless, were recorded in 1882 by Gardner T. Lawton and William Mills. Henry Boyle, John Boles, Dealice Corsen, H. Hodges and Charles E. Huff located the **Independent** and **Yank Boy**. A claim that does not appear in the county index today is that of the **Excelsior,** just outside Old Denny, made by Henry Boyle.

5. In 1883 other new finds included the **Leora** by Smith B. Brooks; the **Mary Blaine** and the **White Elephant** by Brooks and Joseph M. Francis; the **Ellen** by William Mills and Lars Robinson. According to the Trinity County index, Stephen Sherwood's five mines were recorded in 1883.

6. Alice G. Jones *et al,* "Site 48. Old Denny-Mary Blaine Mountain Mining District," *Trinity County Historical Sites* (Weaverville, CA: Trinity County Historical Society, 1981) p. 259.

7. The **Tough Nut** was located by T. J. Baker. The **Red Jacket** was located by Thomas E. Knight, Warrin Watkins, and H. W. Wondesforde, who also claimed the **Argo** and the **Ajax.**

8. See note 5 above.

9. The 1884 new mines in Trinity County were recorded by these men:

John Boles	the **Eureka**
Henry Boyle	the **Rocky Point**
John Clifford & R. L. Thomas	the **High Tone**
John Clifford	the **Mary Blaine no. 2**
George Dean	the **Stella**
George Dean, Frank Duff, George Fisher, W. R. McDowell,	
W. J. McNamara	the **Claremont**, the **Oro Fino**
James S. Davis	the **Thunder Bolt**
Charles Huff, J. C. McCollough	the **North Star**
T. J. Baker, Wallace Graves, E. & W. R. McDowell,	
J. M. McCormack, S. P. Sims, Paul Tario	the **Nevada**
John B. Motherwell	the **Tom Tom**
John McCollough, John S. Sheehy	the **May/Mary Bell**
S. (Steve) Noble, M. Patterson, E. E. Sheffield	the **New York**
Steve Noble	the **Gilt Edge**
A. D. Ritchot	the **Huntington**
James Sinclair	the **Big Chief**, the **Trinity King**
F. S. Shaw	the **Inez May**
R. C. Singer	the **Mountain Chief**
George C. Sarvis	the **Occident**, the **Orient**, the **Argonaut**.

10. *Trinity Journal,* July 18, 1885: "Receiver's Sale.-- At the sale of the property of the Mountain Boomer Company, on Wednesday last, the entire property was bid in by Messrs. Ladd & Clements at $7650. This would indicate that these gentlemen yet have much faith in New River."

11. The owners of new mines claimed in 1885 were:
John Berry, H. A. Libby, Christopher Luther, H.S. Soule the **Luther;** Thom Beard, T. M. Brown, J. P. Haynes, W. W. Webb the **Big Blue**, the **McCracken**, the **Humming Bird**, and the **Celeena;** J. H. Colby the **Rocky Point**, the **Key Stone**, the **Dread Not**, and the **Holy Terror;** John Campbell, Harry Smith the **Mustang;** Samuel Chreston, J. V. Healey (G. V. Hely) the **St. Elmo**; H. Crall the **Hidden Treasure;** James S. Davis the **Pony Creek Boomer;**

Frank S. Duff, George Dean, George L. Fisher:

	the **D. R. Jones** and **George L. Fisher**;
Henry Deoney	the **Eastern Star**;
William Delaney	the **Cape Horn**;
F. Gibson, W. Graves	the **Bald Eagle**, the **Key Stone**;
C. J. Hildreth	the **Live Oak**;
C. T. Hardin	the **Rocky Rim** (placer mine);

Thomas E. Knight, Warrin Watkins and H. W. Wondesforde the **Argo**, the **Ajax**, the **Red Jacket**; H. A. Libby, Christopher Luther, H. S. Soule the **Pierce**, the **Rosina**..

12. Henry Degrooter, *Glossary of Terms Commonplace among the Miners of California: Report of the State Minerologist, State of California,* vol. 1, 1881, p. 280: "Adit: A long, narrow, nearly horizontal opening leading into a mine. In this country the term is usually synonymous with tunnel, though the latter, strictly speaking, means a passage through a hill and is open at both ends."

As for the mystery of the mine's name, Steve Paine, who owns Cinnabar Sam's Restaurant in Willow Creek *(see page 157)*, knows the terrain and the history of New River and has Nellie Ladd photographs lining the restaurant walls. This photograph of the two adits, which is also in the restaurant, is labeled "the Monmouth Mine," but there is no such mine mentioned in any records or articles about the upper New River area.

13. They wrote in old store ledgers, just as the boys had done during their school days *(see Chapter I, pages 22 and 23 above)*.

14. *Trinity Journal,* Dec. 12, 1891. The stories of the ditch and the flume may have been the same construction process.

15. *Mining & Scientific Press,* Jan. 24, 1885, p. 53.

16. Florence E. Morris, "Upper New River: A Tale of Three Cities," *Trinity 1970* (Weaverville, CA: Trinity Co. Hist. Soc, 1970) p. 27.

17. The Boomer arrastra was built in 1883. A 33-foot water wheel was built to turn the arrastra until the stamp mill was built to run it.

The modern spelling of the word "arrastra" comes from the Spanish word "arrastrar," meaning to drag. The mortars of the turning arrastra are dragged over the rock to crush and separate the gold-laden ore. The New River miners and the San Francisco and Weaverville press used the word with a single "r," "arastra," in articles during this 1880s and 1890s gold rush.

18. Morris, "Three Cities," p. 29.

19. See note 18.

20. The June 2003 research expedition located heavy rocks with holes that had once held the cable for the arrastra. The crew did not find all of the arrastra. The Ridgeway Mine also used the Boomer arrastra for some time, bringing its ore to it until developing its own on-site equipment.

21. Morris, "Three Cities," p. 25.

22. *Mining & Scientific Press,* Jan. 24, 1885, p. 53. See a definition of "adit" in note 12 above.

23. Jones, p. 259.

24. Smokey Bergstrom, conversation with the author April 9, 2002.

25. Jones, p. 259.

26. *Trinity Journal,* Sept. 23, 1911.

27. Jones, p. 259.

28. *Mining & Scientific Press,* Jan. 24, 1885, p. 53.

29. Jones, p. 259.

30. Steve Paine of Cinnabar Sam's Restaurant in Willow Creek, CA., conversation with the author June 5, 2002 *(see note 12);* Gay Berrien, e-mail correspondence Nov. 29, 2003.

31. Though the name "Hong" is mentioned by Jones, p. 261, Gay Berrien notes that one important source for this information was Grover Ladd's oral interview of 1965, transcribed, most likely incorrectly, that is, "Hong" rather than "Haun" or "Hahn." Grover stated that there were Chinese miners at the Uncle Sam and the Sherwood, but not the Cinnabar. The *California Journal of Mines and Geology,* volume 37 (1941), quoted in the text identifies Charles Hahn. The *Trinity Journal* states on July 25, 1931, "E. T. Haun has completed the roasting furnace at his Cinnabar mine in the New River district, Trinity County, sixteen miles from Cecilville. The furnace has walls of cement one foot thick and is lined with fire bricks...The mercury or 'quick' will be shipped to Cecilville in the regula-

tion quicksilver flasks of iron by the McBroom mule train which has carried all the supplies to the mine."

32. Holland, transcribed interview with Grover Ladd, 1965.

33. See note 4.

34. *Trinity Journal,* Jan. 10, 1885.

35. *Mining and Scientific Press*, Jan. 24, 1885, p. 53.

36. Gay Holland, transcribed "Conversation with Grover Ladd," 1965. Grover also noted that the tramway system at the Ridgeway Mine was 5000 feet long.

37. The terrain has led majority opinion to conclude that this and the next photograph are of Bob's Farm Mine. The terrain and ridgeline are somewhat similar, however, to those where the Mary Blaine Mine once stood. One opinion comes from Larry McLean, U. S. Forest Service wilderness-minerals technician, who concludes that the terrain fits Bob's Farm Mine and that the lower site (p. 79) is clearly so, though he has never looked for the upper site pictured on p. 78 (Gay Berrien, e-mail correspondence Feb. 3, 2004). On the other hand, Carrol Powell, retired Forest Service culturist in charge of reforestation and timber stand improvement who hunts at Bob's Farm and is very familiar with the area, says neither of p. 78 or p. 79 photographs (Figs. 3-16, 3-17) is of Bob's Farm Mine. He notes that in the photos there is evidence of a fire that left dead trees, and at Bob's Farm today there are huge, unburned trees that would have been evident in these two photos. Powell adds that the ridgeline is different than that at Bob's Farm and is more like that of Mary Blaine Mine. Corroborating evidence for claiming this is indeed a photograph of Bob's Farm Mine is an envelope labeled "Bldgs. at Bob's Farm Mine" which contains a poor negative of the same buildings shot from a different angle.

38. Information about Bob's Farm Company comes from Berrien, Nov. 29, 2003.

39. See note 37.

40. There was a William F. Mann who ran a sawmill in the area.

41. William B. Clark, *Gold Districts of Califonia,* California Division of Mines and Geology, 1970, p. 6, Table 2: "Significant Dates in the History of Gold Mining in California."

42. Howard May, conversation March 17, 2004.

43. Grover is quoted by Gay Holland in "The Tenner Camp," 1971.

44. See note 43.

45. Gay Holland, "The Tenner Camp," *Klam-ity Kourier,* July 7, 1971.

46. Jones, p. 261.

47. The above information was provided by Margaret Wooden, correspondence, Sept. 14, 2002. She also notes the saw handle that is pictured in the hand of the upper man was perpendicular to the saw, as was the handle that the pit man would hold.

48. All the information about the Gun Barrel arrastra ore discharge comes from Morris, "Three Cities." pp. 25-27.

CHAPTER IV

Local Characters & Stories

In a 19th century mining area like New River, history is a mix of journalism, rumor, legend, county records and, in this case, photographs. While in many cases, the stories about local characters are violent accidents, death, and robbery, the less publicized stories, often less violent, are equally interesting. There are community good will stories, unsubstantiated stories considered inappropriate for the local written record, and human interest stories that may not have seemed worth telling to the press 60 or more miles away or writing up if they got there. Nellie Ladd took many photographs of local characters that bring us closer to an understanding of the history made up of these stories about the men, women, children and animals of this mountain mining, trapping, farming and ranching community. There are miners, wives and mothers, children, politicians, animal lovers, trappers, midwives and the mysterious local madame. Like the gold dust in John Huston's Humphrey Bogart film, *The Treasure of the Sierra Madre,* the wind has carried away the promise of gold that brought miners to extreme measures and consequences.[1] But the traces that remain in Nellie Ladd's photographs are rich reminders of a unique local history.

Alex Boyd's photograph is the image of mining itself. Apt for the rough and rugged lifestyle of the miner and trapper, scrambling over the rocks in heat and snow looking for game and gold, he was said to have, as well, a great sense of humor. "Old Boyd," he called himself.[2] The *Trinity Journal* described Boyd as "a jovial soul, ever ready with a good joke on himself or his friends."[3]

From the late 1890s until his death in 1918, he worked placer claims on Emigrant Creek. He may have been a neighbor of the Martins (until 1908) and later the miners at Robber's Roost.

> "Mr. Boyd has worked constantly for a number of years and spared no pains in developing this mine and making it what it is to-day, a valuable little piece of property."[4]

Acommunity man, Alex ran the Ladd store and post office in the absence of Tom Markham in 1894,[5] and in 1902 he was ballot clerk at the election held at the Larcines' hotel.[6] Heading up one winter afternoon in 1918 to check a bear trap only about two miles from his cabin, he stayed out too late and became confused in the darkness. He went the wrong way going home and fell several times in the dark, ending up on Three Creeks. Willard, Grover, and Frank Ladd and others formed a search party that discovered Boyd's body. Willard wrote in his report to the coroner that Boyd went along Three Creeks "about one-fourth mile, where he, given out by his struggles and tumbles, stretched himself out on the bank of the creek and there perished."[7] He was either 81 or 84 years old when he died.

Fig. 4-1. (Nellie Ladd) Alex Boyd in Old Denny. c. 1908.

Mary Blaine, famed mystery madame of Mary Blaine Meadow, left no trace behind--no photographs, no story of her origins or her demise, no home, no newspaper accounts until long after her death. Nevertheless, this madame or prostitute and "road house keeper" meant enough to her community that locals named the peak above her establishment, the meadow and later the mine near it all

Fig. 4-2. (Grover Ladd?) Nellie Ladd (dark dress, light buttons) and friends on an outing to Mary Blaine Meadow. Top left: **Kate Irving, then Mrs. Bert (Sarah) Brackett.** Top right with a snowball: **Jim Irving. Next to him may be Mrs. Byers. c. 1915.**

after her. Only in 1937 were the woman and her profession presented in the *Trinity Journal* and the U. S. Forest Service *California Ranger, Region Five* newsletter (San Francisco), inscribed "not for publication."[8]

A successful businesswoman, Mary Blaine was also kind and generous, "an air of Godliness ever present" in her establishment,[9] with occasional sermons by visiting preachers and an American flag outside. She was known to grubstake miners in need and thus came to hold large interests in many of the richest mines in the area. Rich in gold dust and money from those who paid their way, she gave good business to the White Rock store. But her wealth made her vulnerable to greed and perhaps the drunkenness of her road house company, and she and her gold disappeared. Her mining interests were never cashed in.

Peter and Celina Larcine and their daughter Mary arrived in the New River mining district in 1884, when Mary was just under a year old. All three have continued to capture the hearts of local folks in both Trinity and Humboldt counties over the decades.

Peter was from Tallahassee, Florida, of French heritage, and worked as a cook in Eureka before coming to New River. He was known to tell his friends that when he was broke they could call him Larsen but when he had money he was Larcine. He operated the hotel and a store in Marysville with his wife Celina during the 1880s and 90s. Then he discovered and mined the Cinnabar Mine, where he discovered both cinnabar and silver, and the Utica, a gold mine with a 14-inch ledge and a 600-foot long pay chute on the ground's surface.[10] When he died in 1907, the *Trinity Journal* described him as "a good man in every respect, honest and just in his dealings with his fellow men, kindly and hospitable, a devoted husband and affectionate father...good old 'Pete' Larcine."[11] Today, Steve Paine *(p. 157)* has created a fictional character, based on Peter Larcine, whom he calls Cinnabar Sam. Paine owns a busy restaurant by that name in Willow Creek, in Humboldt County.

Celina, a Missouri-born woman and "the first white woman in the New River mining camp," was said by Nellie Ladd to have caused miner Pony Brown to run out of his cabin, weeping with joy, at her approach.[12]
But the Larcine family's arrival had been fraught with danger: The pack train with which they traveled stirred up a large nest of yellow jackets and caused the mules to panic; fearing for the safety of her 11-month-old daughter, Celina threw the baby "up into a large patch of brush for safety, where she was afterwards picked up smiling."[13] As an innkeeper, Celina always gave a helping hand, nursing sick miners as well as feeding them. In 1895 she invited all the "old bachelors in camp" to a Christmas dinner: "A most delightful repast was served on the occasion, which made some of us think of our far off eastern homes and mothers."[14] She was also a "persistent and...successful prospector."[15] According to the *Trinity Journal*, she studied mineralogy and had several locations (mine sites) she proposed to develop. She owned the Utica Mine with L. Brown in 1908.[16] Suffering from stomach hemorrhaging as early as 1912,[17] she died in 1915 *(see page 32)*.

Mary Larcine was the namesake of Marysville, which was named and mapped by her father in 1885. The *Trinity Journal* called her "a bright and winsome girl."[18] Newspaper accounts discussed her birthdays, her superior skiing, her ski jumping off the hotel roof, her excellence at horseback riding, and her town hall decorations.[19] She grew up with Grover Ladd, four years younger than she, and Willard, a bit younger still. They partied, played, and studied together. Unfortunately, she was a local tragedy as well. "Very sick with a sore throat" in May of 1900, she died the next February 3, 1901, at the age of 17.[20]

Fig. 4-3. (Nellie Ladd)
The Larcine Hotel in Marysville. Porch, L-R: **Frank Ladd, Hazel Dulion, Mrs. Dulion, possibly Eugene Brackett, unknown, Peter Larcine.** Note edge of white skirt far right, which in another print of this scene can be seen to be that of Celina Larcine. Ground, L-R: **Jack Martin, left; Bert Brackett, fourth; Willard Ladd is far back fifth, next to John Hennessey** (flower in his lapel)**; Grover Ladd, second from right, in front of Mrs. Dulion.**
c. 1905.
Glass slide.

NOTE: The small building to the left seems to match the height and shingles of the structure on the far right of the "Hollyhock Walk" photograph, page 56. See also a modern-day comparison, page 154.

97

Stephen Sherwood *(photograph, page 59)* was instrumental in putting the New River mines on the map, giving the area national attention. His five mines, discovered in 1882 and apparently recorded in 1883, created quite a stir in prospecting circles, offering renewed hope of gold in California. Originally a lead miner from Pennsylvania, where he was born in 1810, he was known particularly for his silver finds in Pioche and Meadow Valley before coming to the Trinity Alps.[21] Sherwood figured out that the vein of gold in the Shasta area 100 miles north of Sacramento, an east-west vein, might crop up again at the high point of the Trinity Alps mountains about 60 miles to the west. Making his way up the streams to Mary Blaine peak, he found what he was looking for at the headwaters of Battle Creek. On Sept. 30, 1882 the *Trinity Journal* reported, "The whole hill seems to be a network of gold-bearing ledges. It has been named Gold Hill...Mr. Sherwood has gone to the City to make arrangements to have his ledge developed next Spring."[22] Sherwood brought back with him a San Francisco "expert," Mr. F. E. Jones, who was "highly pleased with all the ledges he saw."[23] By September of 1883, Stephen Sherwood had "men of capital" invested in the Sherwood Ledge, which ran night and day.[24] The Sherwood was powered by both water and steam. When water became scarce, operations switched to steam, requiring the labor-intensive cutting of timber. Thus it was one of the most consistent operations in the area. A mill combining two single stamps into a two-stamp mill, built in 1892, processed the ore until a road was built, under the direction of John Hennessey, to connect the Sherwood and other mines to the ten-stamp Ridgeway mill. *(See pages 77 and 158).*

Fig. 4-4. (V. Budig-Markin) Grant Davis observes ruins of the two-stamp mill at the Sherwood Mine site. July 15, 2002.

Willis Sherwood, one of Stephen's 17 children, came to New River from Illinois at about the age of 22. He joined his father and was probably going to take over the mining operations. They discovered two new ledges east of the Sherwood in 1892, working them all through the winter of 1892-1893.[25] But news accounts in 1893 mentioned Stephen's poor health and a visit to relatives in San Francsco; his mine appears on the delinquent tax list in June of the same year.[26] Then in the horrible Fourth of July accident in 1893, Willis was firing off salutes on the morning of the Fourth with dynamite and held one stick too long. The dynamite exploded, mutilating his hands to the extent that they were amputated by a doctor in Etna who was unable finally to save his life. The young man, only 24 years old, died 27 hours later of internal injuries.[27] His father was sickened with grief and poor health in the spring of 1894, even as he planned development of a new ledge. He died that summer, at the age of 84, and was probably buried next to his son in the White Rock cemetery. *(See page 160.)* The Sherwood Mine had produced $150,000 worth of gold from 1885 to 1894.[28]

Orin Parker Sherwood, Willis's brother, was most likely the "Mr. Sherwood" photographed by Nellie Ladd.[29] A native of Illinois, like Willis, he was born in 1840. He moved to White Rock, purchased part interest in the family mine and operated the stamp mill when District Attorney Jim Bartlett became its principal owner and brother John Bartlett its manager in 1896. There was plenty of water, and nine men were employed at the mine at that time.[30] A concentrator was purchased for the mine in 1903, improving its productivity.[31] A versatile man, Orin was also Justice of the Peace in New River.[32] In 1904 he sold his interest in the mine to now Judge Bartlett and moved to Weaverville, where he died of heart failure in January of 1905.[33]

Fig. 4-5 (Anon.) Orin Parker Sherwood.
Date unknown.
Courtesy of Grant Davis.

Fig. 4-6. (Nellie Ladd) "Mr. Sherwood." c. 1900.
Self-titled.

Frank Ladd, one of the most successful New River mining residents, is a character we see from the perspective of mining and rare travel reports in the newspapers, interviews of his son Grover, and an odd mixture of poses and company in Nellie Ladd photographs. A relentless prospector, he continued to mine and search for new ledges of gold for decades, even while supervising retail sales, pack train operations, and postmaster duties. He came to be known as the father of New River and his name was synonymous with the town of (Old) Denny itself.

Fig. 4-7. (Nellie Ladd) Nellie's husband Frank Ladd at the Denny Store. July 27, 1920.

In 1898 Frank's father, **Frank Ladd, Sr.**, came all the way from Maine to California to visit his son Frank in New River and another son in Chico. He spent the summer in New River with his family and participated in the Fourth of July preparations and celebration, one day he would certainly never forget.

1898 brought war to the United States, and even in the far reaches of upper New River, residents looked at the issues as U. S. citizens. The "New River Items" section of the *Trinity Journal* on June 25, for instance, tells us, "**O. P. Sherwood** is looking as well as usual, he comes to the post office every mail day regularly to get the war news."[34] Thus it was that the Fourth of July, 1898, was a particularly big and patriotic holiday. Taking time out from the "rushing business" at the Denny Store,[35] Frank and his father joined in the festivities.

Though stating that "the Fourth passed quietly at New River," the *Trinity Journal* recounted a sobering story that recalled **Willis Sherwood**'s fatal accident in 1893 *(see page 99)*. At dawn on July 4, 1898, the "very patriotic" Frank and his father were already lighting their "double-headed Dutchman" firecrackers.[36] Unfortunately, Nellie's husband Frank forgot to open the window first, and before he could do so, the firecracker exploded in his hand, blowing a good-sized hole in his hand. Meanwhile, his father was laying one down and it too exploded, taking with it his thumb nail. Both were said to be recovering "as well as can be expected."[37]

Yet another explosion had just missed killing **W. F. Mann** in 1895. Preparing two gunpowder blasts at the Mountain Boomer, he failed to get the second to "spit fire" and left while the first exploded. But as he returned to the site the second exploded unexpectedly. Small rocks riddled his body but spared his eyes and his life.[38]

Willard **Ladd** returned safely from World War I. He was known locally as the cook at the "hotel" or cookhouse in the new town of Denny from the 1930s to the 1950s, maintaining his sourdough starter for some 25 years. During the Depression the Denny cookhouse was alive with miners from McAtee Bar, the Hazel D, the Index and other nearby claims, and Willard would cook for two sittings, of both breakfast and dinner, for the miners. Willard had the bedroom above the kitchen, and mine foremen often rented the other three bedrooms.[39]

Unlike his brother, Willard loved to travel and visit friends. In San Rafael, California, some 300 miles southwest, he visited the Hollands, telling young Gay stories that sparked her interest in the cultural history of upper New River.

Fig. 4-8. (Dick Holland) Willard Ladd, Mariette Nutsch (Gay's grandmother)**, and Gay Holland. July 1, 1952.** (This was Gay's sixth birthday, which was also Grover's 65th birthday.)[40]

101

Grover Ladd had the most stories to tell of all the Denny and New River residents. Gay Holland (Berrien) transcribed a series of Grover stories in 1965, the "late 60s," and 1971. Grover died the last day of 1972 at the age of 85, hardly ever having traveled beyond the limits of the range of the pack train in and out of New River. Here he tells the story of packing whiskey in to the mining towns:

"We packed two kegs of whiskey on a mule which was a pretty good load, I think they were probably 15 gallons, about 300 lbs...They would just draw it out of a keg behind the bar there as far as I know into a bottle. When the keg was empty then get it refilled. Tapping the barrels? A lot of them we were packing had a little gimlet--small--just about as big as a ten penny nail, they would bore a hole down in there on the top and they would drive a small pipe in the side of the barrel and it would run out while they got what they wanted out of it and they just plugged them up, take a little stick and whittle a little plug, and drive in them holes and close them up and then drive the hoop back down over it and they couldn't see it. Put some dirt over the plug on top and smooth it over so it wouldn't show. Then about the fellow who broke the barrel open, a fellow said he took one back over to Callahan someplace and he broke the lid in for some reason, said there was so many pegs drove in there it looked like a porcupine inside. Packers always had their whiskey then. Oh yeah, I heard them old packers, said they just threw a pack cover over a dish pan or something and draw it out and if somebody came, they couldn't stop it and if they took the pan away they lost it. If the boss came around that was lost."[41]

Fig. 4-9. (Anon.) Grover Ladd in (new) Denny. c. 1930 or 1931.

Grover Ladd also told a sad story about a child named Nellie Larkin, who died on the trip out from New River to Eureka in about the winter of 1890. Her parents were leaving the area and had made it the eight miles down to Virgin Creek, where the water was high:

" This fellow was going across Virgin Creek and had (he was riding a mule) a little baby wrapped up in his overcoat under his arm and the mule stumbled in the creek and fell down and the baby slipped out and he didn't know it until he got across the creek and up on the bar there and the baby was gone.

My father went down there several days. He walked from the Boomer down there, looking for her and he finally found her one day, hanging up down there, a mile or two. A little tree had fell out there in the creek and her dress hung up on a snag on it, and they brought her back up there and buried her at old Denny. Nellie Larkin her name was. They were from Eureka. They were moving out.

Bill Murphy that used to be around here, he went back to Weaver, he was related to the Larkins..."[42]

Fig. 4-10. (Anon.) Willard and Grover Ladd in the road. c. 1948.

Grover's stories were always rich in detail and personal experience. He recounted other stories of his father's near death in the avalanche, Jake Hershberger's disappearance, buildings, machines, characters and mines in the Old Denny area, and the fabrication in the wilderness of a pickup from the running gear and clutch of a 1928 Chevy automobile.[43]

Fig. 4-11.
(Nellie Ladd)
Group at the
Boomer
cookhouse.
c. 1905.

Meanwhile, up at the Boomer Mine cookhouse, people posed for a Nellie Ladd photograph in about 1905. Among them are **Jack Martin,** far left, **Bert Brackett**, second from the left, maybe his brother **Eugene** in the center of the photograph (in motion), then **Jim Patterson** fifth from the right, and **Nis Nielsen Brink** second from far right. **Stella Patterson** is in the doorway, then an unknown woman, and next to her little **Hazel Dulion** *(see pages 14 and 97)*, who boarded with the Ladds in order to go to school in Denny. To the right is a tarp (over firewood?) and to the left a basin for hand-washing. A piece of lumber is fastened to a burned stump at the right, which also seen in Fig. 3-14, page 75, holding up a clothesline, or an electric line which would have been operated at this time by the Pelton wheel under the sink in the cookhouse kitchen.

Fig. 4-12. (Anon.) Group photograph at the Boomer cookhouse: Nellie Ladd in doorway between Mrs. Brown and Frank Ladd. c. 1908.

An anonymous Boomer cookhouse photograph in a file at the Trinity County Library, bears the following caption: "Back row--Mrs. Jud Brown, Mrs. Ladd, Mrs. Patterson, Mr. Jim Patterson, Frank Ladd, Bert Brackett, Jerome Hackerman, unknown, Jud Brown, unknown, Frank Noble. Front row--Mr. and Mrs. Hotchkiss, unknown, Willard Ladd, Grover Ladd." See portrait of the Pattersons, page 51, and one of the Hotchkisses, page 53. Everyone is well-dressed, and the Ladd boys seem to have new hats.

**Fig. 4-13.
(Nellie Ladd)
Bert Brackett,
burros and dog.
c. 1912.**

Bert Brackett was an upper New River miner. He and his wife Sarah, whom he married in the fall of 1907,[44] were friends of the Ladds, as were Bert's brother Eugene and his wife. Bert and Sarah were featured in many Nellie Ladd photographs, both together in front of their house with rooster, cats and dog, and on the road with burros. Bert is shown alone with the work animals in Fig. 4-13 in a fog-framed photograph, a humorous shot accentuating both the work of the burros and the playful pose of the dog on top of the load. Textures, activity and local color surround the mountain man.

Sarah E. Biery Brackett, known affectionately as "Little Willie from Downriver" by friends in the area, seems to have been an independent woman, like her friend "Mrs. Jud Brown," with whom she posed in their tomboy dress of overalls and short skirt, respectively. See the photograph Nellie Ladd titled "Mrs. Brown and her short skirt" on page 30, perhaps shot the same day at the Boomer Mine.

RIGHT: **Fig. 4-14. (Nellie Ladd) Mrs. Jud Brown and Sarah Biery**. **c. 1907.**

Sarah met Bert in the eastern United States before the turn of the century and married him in November of 1907. Her good humor was shared with her husband, her women friends and the animals. In an action photograph taken in front of Nellie and Frank's porch in Old Denny, she seems to have just tossed an object in front of a dog, perhaps the same one as in Fig. 4-13 with Bert.

Fig. 4-15. (Nellie Ladd) Sarah Brackett playing with a dog in front of the Ladd home in Old Denny. **c. 1908.**

107

Fig. 4-16. (J. P. Harrington)
Sally Noble. c. 1921. See also Fig. 1-3 and note, page 5.

Sally and Steve Noble were New River residents and the parents of Bill and Frank. Sally, whose mother Polly Dyer was a full-blooded Chimariko and whose father, Joe Joshway, was from Hoopa/Hupa (white or native American), was born either in North Fork or along New River where the Chimariko language was spoken and later Hupa.[45] Steve, who appears to have had some black ancestry, was from Callis, Maine. Steve was among the early prospectors with mines in New River: the Gilt Edge, the Eastern Star, the New York. His mining success made possible the "pretty ranch" seven miles above the mouth of New River where the couple were living in 1897.[46]

Fig. 4-18. (Nellie Ladd)
**Steve Noble. c. 1910.
(Detail, Fig. 4-17).**
See also Fig. 4-22, page 110.

**Fig. 4-17.
(Nellie Ladd)
Steve Noble
and his mule
Rosa at the
Denny Store.
c. 1910.**

**Fig. 4-19. (Anon.) Frank Noble.
c. 1905. (Detail, Fig. 4-12).**

Martha Dyer, Sally Noble's half sister, born in 1866, homesteaded a ranch at the mouth of Bell Creek on New River; her occupation was listed in the 1900 Census as "farmer." She married **Charles B. "Bemay" Zeigler**, born in 1880, who worked with her on the ranch. **George Dyer**, Martha and Sally's brother, worked in various occupations, including running a pack train.[47] The 1900 Census lists George as a placer miner. *(See Appendix B: 1900 Census for New River Township, entries 66-68 and 91-98.)*

Fig. 4-20. (Nellie Ladd) The pack train in Old Denny. c. 1907.

Bill Noble, Sr., Sally and Steve's son, claimed the Eastern Star Mine with his father and **Joe Noble** (see p. 171) in 1885. He married **Rose Clarice Brazille**, from the Forks of Salmon. Rose was native American. She died in 1940. Rose and Bill had four sons and a daughter. According to Grover Ladd, **Bill Noble, Jr.** was called **Tecumseh**, later shortened to "Tumsy," after the Shawnee Chieftain who was a Brigadier General in the British Army in the War of 1812.[48] With His brother **Steve Noble** (named after his grandfather), Tumsy boarded with a family in Old Denny, at the same time Hazel Dulion was boarding with the Ladds, in order to go to school there four months of the year.[49]

Tumsy and Steve's brothers included **Jack Noble**, who moved to Blue Lake, and **Tommy Noble**. The boys' sister **Clarice Noble** moved southwest to Honey Dew. Bill and **Martha Noble** and their children moved down to the Trinity River in the early 1900s before young Bill (Tumsy) fought in the Army in World War I. Tumsy married **Kay Crawford** and had children and grandchildren in Willow Creek, where he was known by residents to have ready candy in his pockets and a smile for all the children.[50] He died in 1970.

Fig. 4-21. Bill "Tumsy" Noble. July 19, 1970. Courtesy of the Willow Creek *Kourier.*

In a Nellie Ladd photograph six men pose in their roles as miners. **Steve Noble** sits at the far left. The man leaning on the building may or may not be **Frank Noble**, Steve's son. **Jack Martin** holds the gold pan.

Fig. 4-22. (Nellie Ladd)
Six New River miners.
c. 1905.

Jack Martin is difficult to identify in general, because he almost always wore a hat shading his eyes. He was most recognizable for his stance, his rifle, and his white gelding. Born in Missouri in November of 1859,[51] he mined in both hardrock and placer operations and lived with his brother **William Martin** on Slide Creek near Emigrant Creek. He appears inside a mine in Figure 63, page 65.

In 1902 the *Trinity Journal* reported the Martin brothers had struck a promising quartz prospect.[52] On January 13, 1908, Jack was driving holes in a boulder to hold dynamite during an Emigrant Creek sluicing operation, when suddenly a boulder loosened from above crashed down onto his leg. The bones were broken and one shattered. Local residents sent for Dr. Mooney in Blue Lake, who came and set the leg well enough for the long journey, beginning January 16, to Trinity Hospital in Arcata, 80 miles away by litter and then by wagon...[53]

Fig. 4-23. (Nellie Ladd) Jack Martin, his white gelding and his big buck, perhaps at the Boomer Mine. c. 1905.

Fig. 4-24. (Nellie Ladd) (L-R) Jack Martin, Eugene Brackett, and friend on the trail. c. 1907.

111

Jack's con- dition wors- ened. By Feb. 3, 1908, Drs. Mooney and McKinnon had to amputate the leg above the knee. A second ampu- tation followed and Jack "rallied from the shock admirably well."[54] But February 25 a blood vessel ruptured in his bowel and he died a day later, at the age of 48.[55]

The tragedy continued. The Martin cabin was a pleasant home on a level clearing above Slide Creek, with twelve-paned windows, out- buildings and even a picket fence. Only three months after his brother died, William went fishing one afternoon and the cabin burned to the ground. The fire, which may have been caused by a spark, took with it the $23 in gold dust that was in the house, leaving melted gold money valued at $5 and some silver, along with one watch. The *Trinity Journal* valued William's loss at $1,000, including the house and its contents.[56]

Jake Hershberger lost his life in the pursuit of gold. Like **Mary Blaine** *(see page 95),* he probably fell victim to lawless greed and was murdered.

Jake was one of the old-timers, mentioned as early as 1883 in the *Trinity Journal,* but may have lived up New River before the hardrock mining craze. Later he lived on Pony Creek. Grover Ladd remembered he "seemed to think he owned the creek; he didn't want anybody else up there."[57] Yet he did come to town and even participated in the elections of 1898 or 1899, captured in a Nellie Ladd photograph showing Jake in the center foreground. This was a period of great local concern for the state of national and international affairs and the war with Spain over Cuba, Puerto Rico and the Philippines. Such was probably part of the discussion at the election, along with the usual stories of gold one also heard around the stove at the Denny Store.

Fig. 4-26. (Nellie Ladd) Elections in 1898 or 1899.
(L-R) **Steve Noble (or Alex Boyd?), Frank Ladd, Bert Brackett, Jake Hershberger in the foreground, an unknown man, Grover behind him, and Jack Martin.**
c. 1898-1899.[59]

But talk of one's gold was a risky affair. Bragging about his gold nuggets one day, and particularly about one worth $80 alone, Jake brought on his downfall. Grover tells the story:

"He had been missing for a month before anybody found out he was gone. They found where he went in the cabin there, he opened a can of tomatoes and ate about half of them and changed his clothes that he had wore down there. He took them off and put them in a wash tub to soak. That's all they ever found out about him. His gun was gone, his coat was still there. Somebody done away with him, it must have happened the same day he got home...Somebody must have followed him in and took the nugget. Never did find him and never will...

Old Jake was a great fellow to talk to himself, sound like there would be 3 or 4 fellows coming and it was only him. We kids could always hear him coming. He was quite a character."[58]

**Fig. 4-27. (Nellie Ladd) John Hennessey
and the Ladd bear cubs.
c. 1912.**

Bears were less a menace than a source of stories and entertainment in New River. The residents hunted bears for fur and meat, and one's first bear kill was an important rite of passage for boys *(see Willard Ladd, page 25)*.

The Ladds also had a pair of bear cub pets that received a great deal of local attention. Nellie took photographs of John Hennessey playing with the cubs and another of Mrs. Cowen feeding a cub from a bottle (it may have been a different animal). Apparently, the cubs became quite difficult to live with. When a tourist passed through the area and admired them, the Ladds gladly gave the cubs away.

Fig. 4-28. (Nellie Ladd) Mrs. Cowen
feeding a bear cub in New Denny.
c. 1912.

115

Grover, Willard and their mother Nellie were particularly interested in several young women who touched their lives: Mary Larcine, who died at the age of 17 *(see page 96)*, Rose Ryan, Belle Irving and Clara Moore, who became Grover's wife in 1936. Nellie took several provocative photographs of Rose, Belle and Clara.

Rose Ryan is pictured in pale ruffled dresses and sometimes a hat, alone, between Grover and Willard, and with dogs in the fork of a madrone tree.[60] She left New River and the boys kept track of her addresses. She was in San Francisco in 1906 and may have experienced the great fire and earthquake that year.[61]

Fig. 4-29.
(Nellie Ladd)
Rose Ryan
with Grover
and Willard
Ladd. c. 1905.

Fig. 4-30.
(Nellie Ladd)
Belle Irving
aiming a rifle
with Grover
Ladd. c. 1903.

Belle Irving lived on her family's ranch at Hawkins Bar and went through school with the Ladd boys. Grover may be holding a hoe or other farming tool in this photograph while Belle practices shooting. As a young woman, she went away to nursing school and became a nurse.

Clara Moore, who cooked at the Tener Camp beginning in about 1916, is captured in Nellie

Fig. 4-31. (Nellie Ladd) Clara Moore poses behind a round of firewood on a burro-drawn litter in the snow. c. 1918.

Ladd photographs alternately working and posed lounging on the grass by the river, but it is clear that she was a working woman. She enjoyed playing with her adopted grandson Bobbie McGregor, working with horses and mules, feeding turkeys. Nellie did not know her for long but captured the charm of this wilderness woman. In 1936 she married Grover Ladd and died in 1952. She was buried in the Denny cemetery *(see pages 141 and 144).*

George Washington Brush Yocom was probably the most distinguished character in New River history and one of the most productive both within and outside the field of mining. A Kentucky man born in 1828, he came to California in the 1849 gold rush and made his fortune first in Placerville, called Hangtown at the time. Moving on and providing the local needs of community after community, he started a store and saloon in Georgetown, a mule train in Nevada City, and a horse-drawn railroad with rails of metal-topped wood connecting Arcata to Humboldt Bay. There he built a wharf to load lumber schooners and transport passengers to Eureka.[62] Yocom was a founder of the Union Wharf Plank and Railroad, which became the Arcata and Mad River Railroad; it extended to the north to Warren Creek (with a locomotive) and east to Korbel. In Hoopa Valley he opened a blacksmith shop and a ferry (with **F. M. Woodward**) across the Trinity River to Orleans Bar. He was also a partner in a flour mill. Displaced by the creation of the Hoopa Valley Indian Reservation in 1865, he and his family (wife **Eunice**, children **Susan** and **George Dryden**) moved to the South Fork of the Salmon River, to a town that came to be known as Yocomville, where Yocom built a two-story hotel and with **Joseph Ritner** a sawmill for a flume providing water to local mines.

Fig. 4-32. (Nellie Ladd) George Washington Brush Yocom (left) **and others between the Ladd home and Denny Store. c. 1895.**

In 1870 the Yocoms moved back to Arcata, where Eunice died at the age of 50. Yocom was remarried two years later, to **Florence Leonard**, with whom he had four children, including Herbert or "Bert." **Bert Yocom** left for New River with his father in 1885. Below old Denny they built a sawmill at Butterfly Flat that was said to be "as busy as the gin mills."[63] Yocom improved the road to White Rock. He became the Denny Postmaster and Justice of the Peace in 1891, giving the service for **Willis Sherwood**'s funeral in 1893. Father and son Yocom dug a mile-long ditch from the Tough Nut to the Hard Tack Mine to "wash the overburden off the rock above the Hard Tack Mine"[64] and developed several hardrock mines: the Blue Moon and later the Monarch and the Overland Cinnabar. He served as Trinity County Supervisor from 1894 to 1898, obtaining funding for two important bridges. He also found time to ski *(see page 121)* and was considered a local expert.[65]

118

Stella Walthall Patterson lived at least three different lives whose confluence surprised many, as recently as the summer of 2002. While New River researcher **Gay Berrien** knew her as Jim Patterson's wife pictured in Nellie Ladd and anonymous photographs in New River, Willow Creek historians knew the couple through Jim Patterson's businesses in Hawkins Bar and his ranch in Willow Creek. **Max Rowley** was the key to the link between Old Denny and Willow Creek, since in 1936 he met the couple in Willow Creek who had been photographed by Nellie Ladd in Old Denny. The Pattersons must have been deciding to separate at the time, for Stella left for San Francisco alone shortly after this. **Margaret Wooden** knew that Jim and Stella Patterson had lived on the ranch on Patterson Road. She also knew Stella Patterson's book *Dear Mad'm* (Naturegraph Publishers),[66] telling about her background in San Francisco, a childhood experience in London, and especially her move in 1953, after a visit to Arcata, to a cabin on a Happy Camp mining claim when she was 80 years old. In the book, Stella confirmed her decision to continue living on the claim rather than return to her family and city life in San Francisco.

Thus it is that San Francisco, London, Old Denny, Hawkins Bar, Willow Creek, Arcata, Happy Camp and its closest city, Yreka, were all part of Stella Patterson's long and active life.

**Fig. 4-33. (Nellie Ladd)
Mrs. Patterson (detail,
Fig. 2-18, p. 51).**

**Fig. 4-34. (Nellie Ladd)
Mrs. Patterson (detail,
Fig. 4-12, p. 105).**

Fig. 4-35. (Anon.) Stella Walthall Patterson. c. 1955.
Courtesy of Naturegraph Publishers.

The local characters leave us with the news of the day as they pass by the Denny Store woodstove to the post office and back-room bar:

"**Potato Hill?** Well, White Rock was a-booming there and they got out of potatoes early in the spring and they got potatoes from **Whitney & Bennett** Co. at the Forks of the Salmon and they had to pack it over there in the snow and there was a big snow drift there and they had to pack it over the hill on the snow and they called it Potato Hill. That's what **George Smith**--he married **the Bennett girl**, in fact she was the only girl they had--and he told me." -- **Grover Ladd**[67]

"The roughest job I ever undertook, however, was the transportation of two mortar beds and a rockbreaker from the north fork of Trinity to New River. We hauled them over mountains and across gulches where so far as appearances went the foot of man had never trod and along precipices frightful enough to make even a Blondin turn pale. It cost us $1800 to haul them 40 miles. I was glad when it was all over." -- **George Dean**[68] (1893)

"The day after my arrival on entering the store I found a poker game in progress and every man had a revolver on the table in front of him. There was in addition a large dagger which seemed to be ready for use by the first man who could reach it. I offered to bet that there was not a cartridge in the whole armory, but there were no takers. After having given them to understand that I was duly impressed with the fact that it was a tough place (to get into with three feet of new snow on the gound to break a trail through) the game was resumed. The fact is New River is one of the most peacable (sic) mining camps in the State. Nobody has ever had 'a man for breakfast' here yet." -- **"Viator"**[69] (1893)

"**Pony Brown** was an oldtimer, he was in here about 20 years before any of this country was discovered up here. Pony Creek might have been named after him or maybe he was on Pony Creek in the early days and they just called it that. He was an old man when Willard and I were about four, in about 1890, we used to go down and have strawberries with him. He had quite a strawberry patch and the fourth of July we always went down there, for a couple of years we did. He lived there until he got old and they took him to the hospital in Weaverville and he died there. He lived down there at the mouth of Emigrant." -- **Grover Ladd**[70]

"**T. B. Markham**, who during the past five years has been clerking here for **Denny & Bar** Co., while on the way from Callahans a few days ago on snow shoes got lost on top of the Mary Blaine mountain in a dense fog and drizzling snow storm, having got turned around, as it were, when within three miles of his destination. He traveled all day over thirty miles of precipices and ravines, endeavoring to reach some habitation before night, but failed in his efforts. He would have camped when darkness overtook him, but six matches, which was all he had, got wet. When almost completely exhausted from journeying onward in the darkness through brush and brambles, about 9 o'clock his attention was attracted by a faint light glimmering in the distance, which he at first supposed to be a camp fire but on approaching discovered it to be a log set on fire to clear a trail, which he also found and which happily led him to civilization the next day. By this fortunately discovered log fire he camped all night, tired, weary, wet, and worse than all, hungry. The next day, however, by following this newly found trail he reached A. **Brizard's** store at Francis, which is managed by the genial and all around good natured **Mr. McAtee**, who got a good breakfast prepared for him, and also extended him his congratulations on making his escape from the bears and panthers." -- **"Prospector"**[71] (1896)

More talk of the town...

Fig. 4-36. (Nellie Ladd) Hazel Dulion and her mother Mrs. Dulion.[75] **c. 1908.**
See pp. 14, 93, 97, 104.

"**Bill Gray**, he was the first mail carrier, he done that on his own before they had a post office, I guess. He charged 25 cents a letter. He started from Junction and down the Trinity River and on the trail up New River, and made a trip about every week or ten days." -- **Grover Ladd**[72]

"**Steve Noble's little girl** came near being caught by a panther the other day. She was riding along the trail when it sprang at her. the horse jumped and threw her off, and had it not been for their big dog, who grappled with the panther and both rolled down a steep bluff about 300 feet into the river, the girl would undoubtedly have been killed." -- **"Moses"**[73] (1892)

"**One of New River's apt young ladies** went to the store the other day and purchased 50 cents worth of peaches, being the first she had eaten this season she ate so many she made herself very ill. The folks thought of calling a doctor, but as there was none within 50 miles they thought she would be better or worse by the time he could arrive, so they 'let it go at that.'" -- **"New River Jay"**[74] (1898)

"**Mr. and Mrs. Jacobs** while climbing the Mary Blaine mountain a few days ago sightseeing, had quite a lively experience in a rattlesnake den. The party succeeded in killing eight of the monsters, one of which measured 46 inches in length. Mr. Jacobs says he will not leave camp again without a pair of six-shooters."[77] (1908)

"**Supervisor Yocom** has left us for winter. He has gone to Weaverville to help frame our local laws, and perhaps decide as to whether we shall have to fight the mighty nation upon whose possessions the sun never sets, or not. Before his departure he had a very narrow escape from (and if he had not been prepared to die, which in all probablility he was, as he is somewhat of a religious turn of mind) a very sudden unprovided death. While out snow-shoeing he imprudently turned his course down a very steep precipice where the snow only laid 20 inches deep. While going at the rate of two miles a minute his snowshoe caught in a bramble, precipitating him 25 feet headlong down the hillside. As a result he fortunately escaped with a few scratches over the left eye." -- **"Friend"**[76] (1896)

NOTES
CHAPTER IV

1. John Huston, *Treasure of the Sierra Madre,* Warner Bothers, 1948. The Oscar-winning film starred Humphrey Bogart and was filmed mainly in Mexico. From the 1936 novel by B. Traven (Berwick Traven Torsvan). Photograph, this page: possibly Mr. and Mrs. Eugene Brackett, small-format print of a portrait by Nellie Ladd, c. 1900.

2. *Trinity Journal,* Jan. 26, 1918.

3. See note 2.

4. *Trinity Journal,* July 27, 1895.

5. "New River Items," *Trinity Journal,* April 7, 1894. Mr. Markham headed out on skis by way of Sawyer's Bar and Scott Valley to visit the Midwinter "Fair."

6. "Election Boards -- New River," *Trinity Journal,* Oct. 4, 1902.

7. See note 2.

8. "Trinity News," "Story of Mary Blaine Mountain," *California Ranger, Region Five,* vol. viii, no. 36, July 30, 1937.

9. See note 8, "Story of Mary Blaine Mountain."

10. "New River Mines," *Trinity Journal*, Oct. 6, 1906.

11. "Death of P. O. Larcine," *Trinity Journal,* Dec. 7, 1907.

12. Nellie Ladd, "Death of Mrs. Larcine," *Trinity Journal,* March 13, 1915.

13. Ladd, "Death of Mrs. Larcine," 1915.

14. "New River Tidings," *Trinity Journal,* Jan. 11, 1896.

15. *Trinity Journal,* July 3, 1897.

16. *Trinity Journal,* July 18, 1908. This was not Lemuel Brown, who had died in 1896.

17. *Trinity Journal*, June 15, 1912.

18. *Trinity Journal*, July 3, 1897.

19. *Trinity Journal*, Aug. 29, 1891; April 8, 1893; Aug. 20, 1898; Sept. 17, 1898; Jan. 20, 1900.

20. *Trinity Journal*, May 18, 1900; March 16, 1901.

21. *Trinity Journal*, Feb. 25, 1883; *Mining & Scientific Press,* Jan. 24, 1885, p. 53.

22. *Trinity Journal*, Dec. 9, 1882.

23. *Trinity Journal*, Sept. 29, 1883.

24. *Trinity Journal*, Sept. 29, 1883.

25. *Trinity Journal*, Sept. 24, 1892 and Dec. 24, 1892; *Blue Lake Advocate,* Feb. 25, 1893 (called Stephen Sherwood "Thomas" in error).

26. *Trinity Journal*, April 29, 1893; June 10, 1893.

27. "Fatal Fourth of July Accident," *Trinity Journal,* July 15, 1893 (from New River July 7); *Trinity Journal,* July 22, 1893.

28. *Trinity Journal*, Nov. 18, 1893; Feb. 24, 1894; April 7, 1894; July 28, 1894; Feb. 23, 1895.

29. Nellie Ladd's photograph self-titled "Mr. Sherwood" could also have been that of a "W. E. Sherwood" who operated the Mary Blaine Mine in 1908 and may not have been related to Stephen, Willis and Orin. On the other hand, Stephen Sherwood's great-great-grandson's photograph of Orin Parker Sherwood looks remarkably like the Nellie Ladd photograph.

30. *Trinity Journal*, June 27 and July 25, 1896.

31. *Trinity Journal*, Sept. 5, 1903.

32. *Trinity Journal*, Jan. 7, 1905.

33. *Trinity Journal*, Jan. 7, 1905.

34. *Trinity Journal*, June 25, 1898.

35. *Trinity Journal*, June 25, 1898.

36. *Trinity Journal*, Aug. 6, 1898.

37. *Trinity Journal*, Aug. 6, 1898.

38. *Trinity Journal,* Jan. 19, 1895.

39. Gay Berrien, correspondence, July, 2002.

40. Gay Berrien, correspondence, Aug. 15, 2002. Berrien also notes the coincidence that both Willard Ladd and Mariette Nutsch, shown together in this photograph, had the same birthday of January 17 (e-mail correspondence Nov. 29, 2003).

41. Holland, interview with Grover Ladd, 1965.

42. Holland, interview with Grover Ladd, 1965

43. Another account of the automobile in Old Denny comes from William "Bob" Everett of New Mexico, who with his father had built the Holland family cabin on the Fairy D Mine around 1935. It was either Everett and his father who had packed the "pickup" (motor, frame and "necessities") up the trail to Old Denny, or they hired Mr. McBroom to do it, as Grover remembered. Mr. Everett called the vehicle a '29 or "30 Chevrolet. Gay Berrien, unpublished article, "Car at Old Denny--The Real Story (?)", dated Oct. 8, 2002.

44. *Trinity Journal,* Nov. 9, 1907.

45. See page 5 and Chapter I reference notes. Note also that the 1900 Census shows Sally Dyer Noble as full "Indian," while her half siblings, Martha and George, are shown as half "Indian." Their father was Orrington Dyer, of Maine. The information about Sally Noble's father comes from her death certificate (Berrien, e-mail correspondence, Nov. 29, 2003).

46. Trinity County index of records; *Trinity Journal,* July 3, 1897.

47. Gay Berrien, correspondence, Aug. 15, 2002.

48. "Happy Birthday Bill Noble," *Klam-ity Kourier,* July 19, 1970, p. 3.

49. Bill Noble," *Klam-ity Kourier,* July 19, 1970.

50. Bill Noble," *Klam-ity Kourier,* July 19, 1970.

51. Gay Berrien, "Death of Jack Martin, or How It Was to Get Medical Attention in Early Northwestern Trinity," Weaverville Chamber of Commerce *1999 Souvenir Book.*

52. *Trinity Journal,* Jan. 11, 1902.

53. *Trinity Journal,* Jan. 25, 1908.

54. *Trinity Journal,* Feb. 8, 1908.

55. *Trinity Journal,* Feb. 28, 1908.

56. *Trinity Journal,* June 13, 1908.

57. Jake Hershberger is mentioned as prospecting in the New River area in the *Trinity Journal* as early as Oct. 20 and Nov. 17, 1883. The Oct. 20 article, moreover, says he is "formerly of New River in this county, returned on Sunday last from San Bernardino County, where he has been for the past two years working in quartz..." Gay Berrien has spoken with a relative of Jake Hershberger who presently lives in Fieldbrook, near the coast east of McKinleyville, CA. Grover Ladd knew Jake when he lived on Pony Creek (Holland, interview with Grover Ladd, 1965).

58. Holland, interview with Grover Ladd, 1965.

59. There were elections in 1898 at the Larcine Hotel. But Gay Berrien thinks that Grover looks older than 11 in this photograph. Jake Hershberger died in early 1900, so Berrien hypothesizes that there may also have been an election in 1899 attended by this group.

60. See photographs, pages 28 (with the Ladd boys), 50 (with the Ladd family) and 56 (alone in the hollyhocks).

61. From the Denny Store ledger, Grover's notes.

62. Margaret Wooden, "George Washington Brush Yocom--Pioneer, Miner, Politician," *Trinity 1998,* pp. 21-33. All information on this page

except reference to skiing in the *Trinity Journal* (see note 65) comes from this excellent historical article.

63. Wooden, "GWB Yocom," p. 24.

64. Wooden, "GWB Yocom," p. 28

65. *Trinity Journal,* March 25, 1893.

66. Stella Walthall Patterson, *Dear Mad'm* (Happy Camp, CA: Nature-graph Publishers, 1982; reprint 2002 with photograph of the author); ISBN: 0879611316; illustrations, Alice Harvey.

67. Holland, interview with Grover Ladd, 1965.

68. George Dean, quoted in the *Trinity Journal,* Jan. 14, 1893.
Trinity Journal, Nov. 4, 1893.

69. "New River Letter": "Viator's Narrow Escape, Toilsome Journey, Poker and Pistols," *Trinity Journal,* March 25, 1893.

70. Holland, Interview with Grover Ladd, 1965.

71. "New River Gleanings": "Man Lost in the Mountains--What the Miners Are Doing," *Trinity Journal,* April 25, 1896. This article suggests that Grover Ladd may have been mistaken in claiming that his family purchased and began operating the Denny Store in 1894. The *Trinity Journal* first mentions the Ladds operating the store in 1898 (Gay Berrien, e-mail correspondence, Nov. 29, 2003).

72. Holland, Interview with Grover Ladd, 1965.

73. "New River Items," *Trinity Journal,* Sept. 24, 1892. This would have been Clarice Noble; see p. 109.

74. "New River Items," *Trinity Journal,* Sept. 3, 1898.

75. Hazel Dulion went to school with the Ladd boys in Old Denny and is seen with them and Floy Lloyd, the teacher in 1904-1905 in the Nellie Ladd photograph on page 14, Fig. 1-13. We know her father was a miner, an election judge, and an old friend of Bert Brackett. See *Trinity Journal,* Sept. 15, 1906, Oct. 6, 1906 and Nov. 9, 1907. Hazel was one of "New River's apt young ladies," a term used earlier in the *Trinity Journal* article by "New River Jay" (Sept. 3, 1898), along with Mary Larcine.

76. "New River Tidings," *Trinity Journal,* Jan. 11, 1896.

77. "New River Notes" (from the *Blue Lake Advocate*), *Trinity Journal,* Aug. 29, 1908.

CHAPTER V

Panoramas & Bridges

Beyond the fragile communities and mines so quickly come and nearly as quickly gone lies the vast expanse of mountains, gorges, trees, streams and meadows of the wilderness that people sought to master and exploit. Nature fed the newcomers, gave them shelter and drink and powered their mine operations. Even when it seemed to have brought them wealth--and more often it did not--nature held the last card. Nellie Ladd's photographs of the panoramas and bridges around her juxtapose the very big and wild, together with the single, the small and the fragile, sometimes human and other times a single tree or a small bridge in a rugged landscape. They show appreciation and respect for nature's power, and sometimes they challenge it as well. Both the panorama and bridge photographs show a certain grace of composition. Their full range of black to white complements the contrasting elements pictured--bridge, man, animal or tree against snow, river, forest and sky of the wilderness context. These photographs range from Nellie's early to later works.

Fig. 5-1. (Nellie Ladd) Rocky foreground against the Trinity Alps. c. 1910.

Nellie Ladd panorama photographs celebrate the wide expanse of mountain views in the Trinity Alps. In this photograph and the next, the snowy mountain backdrop gives perspective and depth to the foreground, here a dark rocky landscape. White outcroppings and small patches of snow complement dark trees, rocks and shadow in this sharply focused photograph.

This multiple horizon photograph captures the two Trinity Alps peaks, Wedding Cake and Thompson Peak. To the left is the North Fork of the Trinity River. Beyond the right is Mary Blaine Meadow. The mid-range mountains are the Pony Buttes.[1]

126

On a wintry morning, this photograph captures the valley and hillsides of Old Denny. Taken from the direction of the Mountain Boomer Mine, it juxtaposes white snow and dark forest, the scene framed by the whimsical branches of dead trees. A comparison modern-day photograph *(see page 153, Fig. 6-43).* shows the forest has regrown after the deforestation pictured here after the turn of the century. Marysville is over the low pass to the right.

**Fig. 5-2. (Nellie Ladd)
View of Old Denny area
from the south. c. 1912.**

127

Mary Blaine Meadow and Mary Blaine Mountain *(center background)* offer panoramic material for Nellie Ladd photographs over two decades. This shot pictures Grover and Willard Ladd in their early adulthood with their dogs. The original print of this photograph is inscribed, "Old hunting cabin on Mary Blaine Mountain. Elev. about 6500 ft." A spring flows not far to the left (northwest) of this upper meadow cabin. A snowy landscape envelopes the central cabin, people, and animals, comfortable in their surroundings in morning sun and shadows.

Fig. 5-3. (Nellie Ladd) Grover, Willard and dogs at old hunting cabin, Mary Blaine Mountain. c. 1906.

Fig. 5-4. (Nellie Ladd) Grover, Willard and dogs on Mary Blaine Meadow. Lower cabin, left. c. 1906.

Grover, Willard and dogs are pictured again on Mary Blaine Meadow, looking south or southeast.[2] The trail to Denny descends southwest. To the left, a cabin with sunken roof nestled in the trees has different siding than the one in Fig. 5-3, located behind the photographer of this scene. Sharper contrast of black and white and trees framing the scene give this photograph a more dramatic quality. The size of the figures shows their relative insignificance and vulnerability, while their stance shows their ease within the larger mountain context.

An unidentified woman and dog pose for this panorama photograph on a promontory with Pony Mountain in the background.[3] The composition juxtaposes dark rock foreground, black forest middle ground and white snow backdrop. Tree branches frame the wide perspective and lead the eye to both the woman and the landscape behind her. In contrast to the tiny figures in other landscape photographs, the woman here is foregrounded. Well-dressed, hatted, and seated at her leisure, she seems to have domesticated both dog and environment. Nellie selected this photograph for a postcard, pictured above in its actual size. Many of these postcards were sold in the Ladd store in Old Denny. This particular example is much more professional and thoughtfully composed than the earlier frozen landscape postcard pictured on page 26.

Fig. 5-5. (Nellie Ladd) Postcard picturing woman, dog and snowy Pony Mountain. c. 1918.
Actual size.

130

Fig. 5-6. (Nellie Ladd) Hillside panorama and White Rock. c. 1898.

This panorama photograph pictures Mary Blaine Meadow and the buildings of White Rock, far lower right. The spectator's eye follows the bright patch of snow on the hillside and the dark trees and bushes down the slope to the tiny village barely visible below in a clearing. The town of White Rock fits into the scene of clouds, misty hills, New River valley, and the Coast Range to the west. The photograph is at once a cultural-geographical study and an artistic framework. In contrast with the postcard opposite *(Fig. 5-5)*, where foregrounding of human and dog places the accent on those elements, here the interest is more in shapes, contrast, brightness, foregrounding and backgrounding appropriated for artistic expression. White Rock is like an aside to the art of the mountain wilderness.

Fig. 5-7. (Nellie Ladd) Self-titled, "Reflections": White's Creek Lake. c. 1910. Self-titled.

A very different landscape photograph pictures three hunters at what may be White's Creek Lake, on the back side of Pony Mountain, across the East Fork from Old Denny.[4] The three people, two of whom may be women in overalls, pose on a rock with their rifles, light shirts against a dark foliage backdrop. Composition is the key to the photograph. Two-thirds of it is a reflection from the lake, capturing more than the scene reflected, including tall trees, the hilltop, and even something on the rock just above and left of the people. The visual image in the reflection of the scene, like photography itself, reveals more than its model.

Contrasting with the water of "Reflections" *(Fig. 5-7)* is the dry riverbed accentuated in this photograph of the bridge over the Salmon River at Forks of Salmon. Three people pose on the bridge, with its natural and pole supports, against the lighter distant mountain. At least one other person looks up at the bridge near a bridge support pole. A curious dog sniffs the riverbed rocks in the distant foreground. The artistically-shaped driftwood, lower right, leads the viewer's eye to the center of the photograph and the outcropping that supports the bridge. The river itself, probably at its summertime low, is nearly forgotten in the landscape.

Fig. 5-8. (Nellie Ladd) Bridge at Forks of Salmon. c. 1896.

Built in the 1880s, this bridge was eight feet wide with six feet clear. It was constructed according to specifications requiring it be attached to the huge rock in the river.[5]

133

Fig. 5-9. (Nellie Ladd) Bridge over the Trinity River at Hawkins Bar. c. 1904.

The waters of the mighty Trin and a horse in this Nellie ity River are traversed by five people Ladd photograph of the mule bridge at Hawkins Bar. Reflecting waters provide a peaceful frame for a seemingly fragile bridge, its span accentuated by the low angle of the photographer's stance at the river's silty edge. Nellie made a postcard of this photograph. Built originally in 1902, the wire bridge spanned 240 feet between towers and was considered the best bridge on the river,[6] though it was sometimes impassable due to needed repairs. In 1907 the flooring was placed on the upper cable.[7] In 1918 the construction of a new wagon bridge was announced in response to a local petition.[8]

**Fig. 5-10. (Nellie Ladd) Alice Jacobs on the
Hawkins Bar bridge. c. 1903.**

Alice Jacobs, here a teenager, figures in the New River story beginning in 1903. This pale Nellie Ladd photograph may commemorate her arrival. "Jakie," as she was known by her friends, may have worked at the Tener Mine and there befriended Clara Moore, Grover Ladd's future wife, during the period from 1913 to 1918, when she would have known Nellie Ladd as well. She became very close to Clara's grandson and adopted son Bobbie McGregor Moore. When "Jakie" moved to Salyer and later to Eureka, she watched lovingly over Bob and Mary Moore's children. She was a friend, not only of the Ladds, but also of Kate and George Irving and their children, who lived not far from this bridge. *(See bridge, page 134 and the Moore-Jacobs story and more recent photos, page 141.)*

A newer wire mesh mule bridge connects the shore with a live oak tree to a tree-covered dark hillside whose rocks fall in a gentle curve into the low-flowing river. The people on the bridge are barely visible in front of the fading distant forest. Photographic historian Jeff Buchin believes the site could be the mouth of Plummer Creek, where it flows into the South Fork of the Salmon. Far up this stream is the site of the Gun Barrel Mine. In 1906 Frank Patten built a trail over into the Salmon River drainage to the Gun Barrel Mine, a trail that the Ladds later continued to Plummer Creek.[9]

Fig. 5-11. (Nellie Ladd) Mule bridge, possibly the mouth of Plummer Creek. c. 1910.
Postcard, enlarged.

Also over the Trinity River, several miles upstream at the mouth of New River, a new suspension bridge was built in 1914, thanks to citizens of Lower Trinity and New River.[10] It was constructed by the Larsen brothers to access the New River trail near Gray Creek. By far the most dramatic of Ladd's bridge photographs, this vertical image captures the grandeur of the scene, which was probably the dedication ceremony attended by the Ladds and the Irvings *(see page 19 above)*.

On April 27, 1918 the *Trinity Journal* mentioned a "picnic party" held at the site of this same bridge. That article might also refer to the moment this photograph was taken, which would be four years later:

A picnic party, consisting of Mr. Pettry, who is visiting friends at Hawkins Bar, Misses Pearl Griffith, Kate and Blanche Irving and a few friends from up the river, crossed the foot bridge at the mouth of New River and spent the day on the pretty little flat at the foot of the New River crags. Few people outside our immediate neighborhood know that at the foot of old Ironsides, thence for several miles down the river we have the wildest and most picturesque gorges in the State and that this gorge is spanned by a fine mule bridge, nearly 150 feet above the rushing waters of the Trinity.[11]

Fig. 5-12. (Nellie Ladd) Suspension bridge at the mouth of New River over the Trinity River. c. 1914.

NOTES
CHAPTER V

1. Description of the scene comes from conversations with Gay Berrien, Margaret Wooden and Max Rowley in August, 2002.

2. This winter scene compares to the early summer mule train scene on this meadow on both the title page of this book and page 47. See also "before and after" photographs on page 156.

3. Gay Berrien, conversation, August, 2002 and e-mail January, 2003.

4. Description of the scene comes from conversations with Gay Berrien, Margaret Wooden and Max Rowley in August, 2002.

5. Margaret Wooden, conversation, August, 2002.

6. *Trinity Journal,* Nov. 7, 1903.

7. *Trinity Journal,* Nov. 2, 1907.

8. *Trinity Journal,* Feb. 2, 1918; April 27, 1918.

9. Alice G. Jones et al, *Trinity County Historical Sites*, Trinity County Historical Society, Weaverville, CA, 1981, p. 261.

10. *Trinity Journal,* March 13, 1915.

11. *Trinity Journal,* April 27, 1918.

Fig. 6-1. (VBM)
Frank Wallen (Jr.) on
the ranch. 2000.

CHAPTER VI

New River Today

Trinity Rose Pellegrini.
Detail, Fig. 6-40 (p. 152).
2003.

Starting up New River today from the Trinity River at Hawkins Bar, one passes by small farms, ranches and orchards nestled in the valleys. One ranch is the old Irving Ranch, which now belongs to Frank, Jr. and Virginia Wallen; Frank's brother Charles "Rusty" and his wife Victoria Wallen live on an another parcel of the old homestead.[1] Frank and Rusty are grandsons of Kate and George Irving and sons of Annie *(see Annie Irving on page 17)* and Frank Wallen. Frank (Jr.), Fig. 6-1, knew Grover Ladd, who had always been a family friend, and Frank stayed with Bill Noble at the Ladd bunkhouse in Denny when they went hunting.[2] Even as a child, Frank used to camp out with a 30-30 rifle because of the danger of bears, panthers and bobcats.[3] The Irving Ranch was a favorite stopover for travelers along the journey to and from the mines, and children boarded there to attend school. At one time it had two barns, a blacksmith shop and a saddle house; by 1920 the ranch had grown to 160 acres and supported 100 cattle.[4]

Another stopover for miners heading to Denny was the Dailey Ranch. This valley, dotted with houses and barns, fenced fields, livestock and grazing deer, is the home of woodsman and rancher Jim Pellegrini and his two-year-old daughter Trinity Rose. Jim has helped researchers pack kitchen supplies into Old Denny since 1999. Trinity, pictured above and with her father in Fig. 40 *(page 152),* has already become a New River celebrity after winning the parade trophy riding a mule in the Willow Creek Bigfoot Daze parade on Labor Day weekend in 2003. Her confident smile seems to capture the spirit of the new generation along New River.

Nineteen miles up the winding road from Hawkins Bar, the new Denny is still a picturesque village in the new millennium. Residents count the population on their fingers and come up with 23. Now a private residence, the present "Ladds Store" was built in 1932. The old store burned down in 1929 when Frank Ladd went out one day to feed the chickens and the curtains caught fire.[5] Out in front the Fire Chief gasoline pump rusts in the rain, and the few vehicles that pass by on their way to homes, trailheads or fishing holes usually fail to stop at the stop sign, which reads "WHOA." The U. S. Forest Service maintains a campground nearby.

Fig. 6-3. (V. Budig-Markin) Old fuel pump at the "Ladds Store" in new Denny. 2001.

Photos © Valerie Budig-Markin

Fig. 6-2. (V. Budig-Markin) The new Denny and the "Ladds Store." 2001.

Grover moved down to new Denny in 1920 to begin the three-year homesteading process for the family, a process he completed a year after Nellie died, in 1923. Frank Ladd died in 1932. Grover married Clara Moore, who became the Denny Postmaster, while her husband ran pack trains and hired ranch boarders. Willard was the chief cook at the "cookhouse" or "hotel." Gay Berrien remembers the strong smell of butter and Willard's sourdough pancakes. A man who loved to travel, Willard visited the Dick Holland family (Gay's parents) in San Rafael, near San Francisco, when he was traveling through the area[6] *(see page 101)*. Willard died in 1960.

Clara Moore's grandson Bobbie (McGregor) Moore was orphaned in Nevada when he was 5 or 6 years old, and he was adopted in Reno by Clara in about 1926. Bobbie went to school in Burnt Ranch (teacher Jenny Irving), home schooled in Denny with his grandmother/mother, went to school in Adin, and in the 7th grade started going to school in Eureka. After high school, Bob went to work in Eureka, then went to Reno, where he joined a magazine crew. His job took him all around the U. S., and he met Mary, his future wife, who accompanied him back to Denny to help Clara build her house.[7] (Clara's brother S. C. Moore built the Ladd bunkhouse in 1941.[8]) Bob and Mary Moore lived in Eureka, where Bob worked for Levi-Zentner Produce, and after retiring and traveling, moved to Apache Junction, Arizona.

Fig. 6-4. (Grover Ladd) Bobbie and Clara Moore with Grover's collie.[10] **c. 1927.**

Their son Michael and Catherine Moore live in Eureka today. Michael remembers going to Denny in 1952 for Clara's funeral and meeting Grover, who made him a sluice box and took him panning for gold.

**Fig. 6-5. (Anon.)
Bob and Michael Moore.**
Bob's 80th birthday, **Dec. 29, 1999.**
Courtesy of the Michael Moores.

Michael Moore's grandmother figure Alice Jacobs, who came to Denny in 1903, according to the Moores, is pictured around the time of her arrival as a teenager on the new Hawkins Bar bridge over the Trinity River on page 135, Fig. 5-10. She may have worked at the Tener Mine with Clara, then moved out to Salyer and then to Eureka.[9]

**"Jakie":
Detail,
Fig. 5-10,
page 135.
c. 1903.**

**Fig. 6-6. (Anon.)
Alice "Jakie" Jacobs. c. 1980.**
Courtesy of the Michael Moores.

Across the street from the store, cookhouse/hotel and bunkhouse in Denny is Grover and Clara Ladd's home. When Clara died in 1952, Grover lived alone in the house until 1958, when Frank and Evelyn Gifford's cabin burned down in Denny. Though the Giffords also lived in Trinity Center, where Frank had a molding mill, Grover invited them to stay until they rebuilt their house in Denny. They stayed on and sold the new house. Grover died in 1972, Frank Gifford in 1973, and Evelyn a few years later.[11] Their son Lowrie "Giff" Gifford lived in the house until he died in 2001. In 2000 he spoke kindly of Grover. It was Lowrie who offered Grover's collection of Ladd photographs to the Trinity County Historical Society.

Fig. 6-7. (V. Budig-Markin) Grover and Clara Ladd's ("Giff's") house. 2000.

Fig. 6-8. (V. Budig-Markin) Lowrie Gifford at the house in Denny. 2000.

Grover's cherries impressed both Michael Moore and Gay Holland Berrien as children. Grover loaned his friends, the Dick Holland family, his mule Pedro for their family outing up New River in 1951 and put a sack of cherries on the side where three-year-old Eddie was riding as they set off. When the family arrived at their destination at their mining claim on Slide Creek, Eddie was a very sick little boy and the cherries were gone.[12] Michael's memory of Grover's cherries probably came originally from 1952 and his great-grandmother Clara's funeral.[13] The Ladds had other fruit trees in the garden as well.

Dick Holland's first trip up New River was in 1939. Shortly after that he brought up his wife Marietta by motorcycle. They bought a placer mining claim along Slide Creek, and in the summer of 1951 the Holland family--Dick, Marietta, and their four children, Chuck (8), Gay (5), and Eddie (3), pictured, and Rich, who was 16 or 17 years old, took a trip from above the new Denny up the same trail the 19th century gold miners once followed. This was the first experience of New River for Gay, her first lesson about the mines, the forest, and the cultural history surrounding them. For many years they vacationed in a log cabin there, constructed with upright logs, until the family bought private land closer to Denny, and then in Denny itself.[14]

Grover never liked to travel much, and as he progressively lost his parents, his wife and then his brother, he particularly appreciated the company of the Holland family in Denny. Grover and Dick were good friends and the two men, according to Gay, had much in common, including high integrity and total honesty.[15]

Fig. 6-9. (Jack Murdock)The Holland family trip to upper New River. (L-R) **Marietta, Gay, Chuck, Eddie, Dick. 1951.** Courtesy of Gay Berrien.

Watching Gay grow up with an increasingly professional interest in the cultural history of the area, Grover gave her interviews and stories about the history of upper New River until not long before his death in 1972.

The 1970s brought the baby boomers to Denny and changed the character of the community. It was a contradictory time of peaceful principles and flying bullets, but history finally came full circle, and Denny became a quiet mountain village again, where the traditional residents and the "rebel group" learned to coexist.[16]

Fig. 6-10. (Ed Holland) Grover Ladd, Dick Holland, and Boots. 1963.
Print from a slide. Courtesy of Ed Holland.

Overlooking a Denny meadow where horses graze by day and deer by night, a mossy oak tree shelters the Ladd graves in a tiny gated cemetery. Frank and Nellie Ladd lie beneath the large upright headstone in the cemetery *(upper photo, right)*, Grover and Clara lie together, near Willard's religious and military grave marker.

Photos © Valerie Budig-Markin

Figs. 6-11 to 6-14. (V. Budig-Markin) Photos of the Denny cemetery. 2001.

Facing the meadow below the Denny cemetery is the home of Smokey Bergstrom, who has many of the Ladd treasures left by Grover. One of these is what may be Nellie Ladd's linen chest, a fragile metal-strapped wooden chest with designed paper lining. It holds lace and starched white apron, tablecloth and other linens. Smokey owns a box of books from Nellie and from Grover, books whose inscriptions, as well as their content, give a sense of important relationships and interests *(see page 27)*. A chest of drawers with a matching carved wood-framed mirror was Nellie's, according to Grover, who talked to Smokey of hauling it up to Old Denny and then hauling it back down to new Denny in 1921. Shot glasses from the Jim Frantz saloon in Old Denny, in a line on Bergstrom's window sill, are much bigger than those used today. Grover tells about big shots of whiskey sold in Old Denny at his parents' Denny Store, across the street from the Jim Franzen Saloon *(see page 21)*.

Not only does Smokey know a lot about the characters and history of upper New River mining, he also has his own story of life in that district. He, his wife Barbara, three other couples and all their children lived at the Tough Nut Mine, next to the Ladds' Mountain Boomer, the Bergstroms and the Codys for 13 summers and 8 winters (1972 to 1980).[17] This mine property is the only private parcel in the western portion of the Trinity Alps Wilderness Area today. In the spirit of the times, these young families believed in a lifestyle of community in mountain solitude, refusing the invasion of a proposed film about their lives. Hot in the summer, snowed in during many winter months, their life was in many ways similar to that of the Ladds nearly a century earlier, making do with what was available and shipping in the

Photo © Valerie Budig-Markin

Fig. 6-15. (V. Budig-Markin) Smokey Bergstrom with the Ladd chest of linens. 2002.

rest over a long distance by horse or by mule.[18] They too dug ditches and constructed buildings, carried water, picked berries and apples, set sourdough starter to rise, and had gardens to till, tend and water. Like the Ladds' first home nearby, the Codys' cabin, too, was hit by an avalanche and filled with rock until eight strong young men helped dig it out.

Darlene Cody and Barbara Bergstrom were wives, mothers, and mine co-owners at the Tough Nut Mine. Both served as each other's midwife and had successful childbirths on the mountain top. Both got up before dawn and began the morning chores: building and stoking the stove fire, grinding grain for flour, setting bread to rise, climbing down to the "refrigerator" mill stream. They were the first in their families to get up in the morning and the last to go to bed. After breakfast they had chores all day, searching for firewood, caring for and teaching their children, picking berries to make jam, canning 365 jars a year of fruit from trees left by earlier inhabitants of New River. They canned meat, grew herbs, vegetables, and sunflowers, cared for chickens and then cooked them. Darlene, who just celebrated her 35th anniversary

Photo © Valerie Budig-Markin

Fig. 6-16. (V. Budig-Markin) Darlene Cody, Barbara Bergstrom at Barbara's home in Redding. 2003.

with Leon in January, 2003, stressed that it was particularly difficult for these modern couples to live in upper New River because they were familiar with the life and modern amenities of the city. Their choice to live in nature was at once a luxury and a burden, knowing as they did how much easier their lives would be with electricity, running water, stores, and schools for their children. As it was, they got school books in Weaverville from Bob Gravette, Trinity Co. Superintendent of Schools, for home schooling, much like Nellie Ladd had done.[19] They had beautiful old cookstoves, always full of cooking pots, and foot pedal sewing machines to make and mend curtains (hand-dyed with plant juices), linens and clothes. Barbara had an old tub washing machine with electricity, after six years without it. Their cabins were always full of drying diapers hanging in the upper lofts where the air was warm and dry. They were religious, worked hard, and stayed healthy.[20]

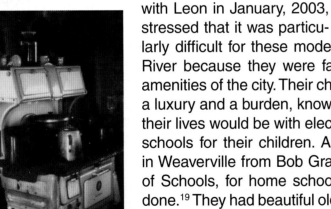

Fig. 6-17. (Darlene Cody) The Cody cookstove. 1975. Courtesy of the Codys.

Fig. 6-18. (Darlene Cody) The Cody sewing machine at the cabin. 1975. Courtesy of the Codys.

Fig. 6-19. (Anon.)
The Bergstroms: Smokey,
Barbara, Hawk, Serena and
Rebecca. 1978.
Courtesy of Barbara Bergstrom.

Fig. 6-20. (V. Budig-Markin)
Barbara and Hawk Bergstrom
at the Tough Nut. 2003.

"Barbara came down to visit one evening," commented Darlene casually at Old Denny in 2002, "and after dinner we went upstairs and birthed a baby. It was such a mellow birth, by kerosene lanterns and candle light." Andrew was born a happy boy, never crying. He slept peacefully the whole first night.

The children lived a great life, swimming, hiking and picnicking, their mothers trying to keep them from falling off cliffs while their fathers were building, repairing, looking for construction materials, and arranging the packing in of supplies. Special treats were the home-made rootbeer cooled in the cave of the Boomer Mine adit (the "Meckel Crosscut"), and in the winter a warm dinner of "Mar-far," venison jerky wrapped in corn dough and fried in the iron skittle. The children survived rattlesnakes, a stumbling mule, and snow storms at home and on the trail, moving with their parents back into town in 1980 for school.

In 2003 the Bergstroms, divorced, have four children and travel to visit each other in Denny, Redding and San Diego. Laurel, born in Weaverville, is 16. The Codys have six children, now-independent, and still live in Weaverville. Barbara travels over the mountain every Sunday to go to church with the Codys, and Barbara and Darlene take time to revisit the mountains together on backpacking trips to the high lakes and meadows of the Trinity Alps. Smokey keeps up the Denny "rebel group" lifestyle.[21]

Fig. 6-21. (Diana Brandt)
The Codys: Leon, Darlene (pregnant with J.R.), L-R: Levi,
Andrew, and Travis. 1978.
Courtesy of the Codys.

Fig. 6-22. (V. Budig-Markin)
Leon, Darlene and Frank Cody
at the Tough Nut cabin.[22] 2003.

Fig. 6-23. (Smokey Bergstrom) The Mountain Boomer stamp mill. 1974. Photo courtesy of Smokey and Barbara Bergstrom.

Fig, 6-24. (V. Budig-Markin) Boomer stamp mill. 2002.

Photo © Valerie Budig-Markin

Barbara Bergstrom took this photograph (left) of the Mountain Boomer stamp mill in 1974. The bottom of the three stamps are just visible. Notice the steep roof slope protecting the original structure from the weight of snow. Grover Ladd used to say that they waited until the snow reached a depth of five or six feet on buildings before going up to shovel them off.[23] By the summer of 2002, however, the stamp mill had fallen down and the three stamps were lying exposed to the weather.

Fig. 6-25. (Nellie Ladd) Workers in the Boomer stamp mill. c. 1910.

Photo © Valerie Budig-Markin

Fig. 6-26. (V. Budig-Markin) Inside Boomer stamp mill. 2002.

148

The first Ladd home, close to the Boomer stamp mill, may have been replaced by a mine building after the Ladds moved to Denny in January of 1890. The Boomer cookhouse was above the Ladd homesite, the arrastra, the stamp and sawmill sites. Today the trail up to these sites is about the same, though much of it has slid, along with some buildings, into the gorges. Two buildings lie in ruin.[24]

A Nellie Ladd photograph (below) taken at the Boomer cookhoouse shows a man zeroing in his rifle; Randy Steinbeck re-enacts the scene about 100 years later in Fig. 6-30. Fig. 6-31 shows the spectacular view westward enjoyed by those of both centuries.

Fig. 6-27. (Nellie Ladd) Up to the cookhouse. c. 1903.

Fig. 6-28. (V. Budig-Markin) Up to the site of the cookhouse. 2003.

Fig. 6-29. (Nellie Ladd) Zeroing in a rifle at the Boomer cookhouse. c. 1905.

Fig. 6-30 (V. Budig-Markin) Zeroing in Randy Steinbeck's rifle. 2003.

Fig. 6-31. (V. Budig-Markin) View from the cookhouse: Barbara Bergstrom and John Palmquist rest after recording site data.[25] 2003.

Fig. 6-32. (Nellie Ladd) One of the Boomer adits, tramway to the Boomer stamp mill. c. 1910.

The Mountain Boomer Mine adits, Lewises' boarding house, and "a large number of cabins"[26] lay across another mill stream from the Boomer stamp and sawmills and cookhouse. A Nellie Ladd photograph shows one of the mine adits directly across the creek from the Boomer mill. Ore from this mine came out on ore cars running on the iron rails of a tramway over the creek, sending gold-bearing rock to the stamp mill and waste rock to create a flat near the mill, useful for mining operations. Researchers in 2003 entered this mine and followed the adit back past an ore car still on its rails, through about 250' of 16-18"-deep water, some 650' into the mountain, where the adit splits into three short forks. Streaks of white calcium carbonate form as ground water drips down the walls. Yew timbers (for hanging lanterns or candles, since the firm rock in the adit did not require timbers for support) and rocks jut down from the ceiling, and old lumber on the wet floor has become oozing mud. Modern visitors found no traces of gold.

Photo © Valerie Budig-Markin

Fig. 6-33. (V. Budig-Markin) Randy Steinbeck (tiny figure outside the adit)**, the ore car just in front of him, and about 100 feet of the Boomer adit. 2003.**

Fig. 6-34. (John Palmquist) Randy Steinbeck, Barbara Bergstrom, and the author outside the adit. 2003. Courtesy of John Palmquist.

150

Fig. 6-35. (Anon.) Nellie at home in Denny. c. 1896.

Photo © Valerie Budig-Markin

Fig. 6-36. (V. Budig-Markin) Site of the Ladd home cellar and part of the porch fir tree. 2001.

Photo © Valerie Budig-Markin

Fig. 6-37. (V. Budig-Markin) The Ladd homesite and foundation rocks. 2001.

The rock wall in front of the tree today can also be seen in the 19th century photograph above, supporting the porch and the house.

The Ladds moved from the Boomer to Butterfly Flat, just outside Denny, in 1890, then into the old Boynton saloon and town hall in Denny in 1894. An anonymous photograph shows Nellie on the porch of her new home. The tree growing through the porch is today a stately fir standing alone near the junction of the New River trail ("Main Street," going west down New River and north to Marysville and White Rock) and the trail south to the Tough Nut and Mountain Boomer. Fig. 6-36 shows the depression that was once the Ladd cellar next to the porch tree, pictured on the left of Fig. 6-37. Imagine the 20' x 50' home extending back into the new green of the forest. (It is a felony for modern visitors to disturb or remove any artifacts from such century-old sites.[27])

151

Fig. 6-38. (V. Budig-Markin) Mule train in Old Denny. 2002.

Fig. 6-39. (Nellie Ladd) Loaded mules at the Denny Store. c. 1907.

Amodern-day mule train stops at the main intersection in Old Denny. The Denny Store was at the photograph's left, behind the tree with the Denny sign. The Nellie Ladd photograph, Fig. 6-39, shows that tree *(left)* and the Ladd mule train in front of the Denny Store. Two men stand on the store porch, perhaps Grover and Willard.

Jim Pellegrini has put a mule team together to help the Old Denny researchers haul in food, kitchen supplies and some personal gear on their yearly expeditions, which are supported by private donations to the Trinity County Historical Society.[28] Jim now has a baby daughter, Trinity Rose, who has made her father blossom as well. She began riding a mule at the tender age of 20 months. *See page 139.*

Fig. 6-40. (Gay Berrien) Trinity Rose and Jim Pellegrini. 2003. Photo courtesy of Gay Berrien.

Fig. 6-41. (V. Budig-Markin) The pack train on the New River trail. 2002.

Sell your books at
sellbackyourBook.com!
Go to sellbackyourBook.com
and get an instant price
quote. We even pay the
shipping - see what your old
books are worth today!

Inspected By: paulino_cervantes

00072277828

Fig. 6-42. (Nellie Ladd) Old Denny area from the south. c. 1912.

Fig. 6-43. (VBM) Old Denny area from the Boomer. 2002.

The landscape of upper New River has changed due to natural reforestation of the wilderness, as one can see in these 1912 Nellie Ladd and 2002 views above of the Old Denny area as seen from the direction of the Mountain Boomer and Tough Nut mines. On the other hand, structures have disappeared and the forest has been devastated by fire, as evident in Fig. 6-45 below. A less populated area than Denny until at least 1913, Robber's Roost maintained its rich forest environment. The modern day photograph shows trees blackened and killed by the 1999 forest fire and all wood structures gone. People stand in the distance near a spring in about the same place along the trail in both the Nellie Ladd scene and the modern photograph.

Fig. 6-44. (Nellie Ladd) Robber's Roost. c. 1915. *(See p. 55.)*

Fig. 6-45. (VBM) Robber's Roost. 2002.

153

Fig. 6-46. (Gay Berrien) Valerie Budig-Markin re-enacts the Nellie Ladd "Hollyhock Walk" photograph in Marysville. 2002.

Fig. 6-47. (Nellie Ladd) Woman in the hollyhocks: "Hollyhock Walk." c. 1905. Self-titled.

Fig. 6-48. (Nellie Ladd) Larcine Hotel, Marysville. c. 1905.

Aflower in the wilderness makes all the difference. Three years after the 1999 forest fire, among the blackened trees just north of the site of what was once the Larcine Hotel in Marysville, there appeared a striking white double hollyhock in full bloom. This flower in 2002 brought together the contexts of two historic Nellie Ladd photographs, one she had titled the "Hollyhock Walk" *(Fig. 6-47 and page 56)* and a group portrait in front of the Larcine Hotel *(Fig. 6-48 and page 97)*. The small building to the left of Fig. 6-48 could very well be the shingled structure on the left of the "hollyhock walk" photograph, Fig. 6-47. At the very top of that photo can be seen what may be the edge of a roof, perhaps that single-slope roof of the structure in the Larcine Hotel photograph. Today's hollyhock bush is about ten yards north of the hotel site and thus right where the young woman would stand in 1910 enjoying the hollyhocks near the hotel. The hollyhocks today are just off the main trail/road from Old Denny through Marysville to White Rock and the northern mines of the district.

Outside Marysville the blooms continue. About 1/4 mile toward Denny, looking back, one sees lavender lupine soft against the black of the burned forest.

Fig. 6-49. (VBM) Lupines outside Marysviille. 2003.

Over the ridge and down north toward Denny, late dogwoods bloom in June in the filtered light.

Fig. 6-52. (Rob Robinson) Dogwood blossom. 2003.
Courtesy of Rob Robinson.

Fig. 6-50. (VBM) Balsamroot and paintbrush, lower Mary Blaine Meadow. 2003.

Up on the western edge of Mary Blaine Meadow is a spring, a campsite, scraggy rocks and a big flat rock where Willard Ladd carved his name in 1915.

Along the ridge southeast of Marysville, one heads up toward Mary Blaine Meadow, filled with yellow balsamroot, paintbrush, and tiny purple delphiniums.

Fig. 6-51. (Rob Robinson) Balsamroot blossoms. 2003.
Courtesy of Rob Robinson.

Fig. 6-53. (VBM) "W. W. LADD 1915" carved on a rock in Mary Blaine Meadow. 2003.[29]

Fig. 6-54. (Nellie Ladd) Grover, Willard Ladd guide the mule train across Mary Blaine Meadow. Pony Buttes backdrop. c. 1907. *(See title page and p. 47.)*

Fig. 6-55. (V. Budig-Markin) Mary Blaine Meadow, with Pony Buttes backdrop. June, 2003.

Seeing the late spring flowers in 2003 helps one better "picture" a similar scene portrayed by Nellie Ladd on Mary Blaine Meadow with the Pony Buttes behind the Ladd pack train (facing southeast). Taken in the spring after melting snow allowed the boys to bring the team back from Callahan, the Ladd photograph shows probably the same little bushes about to flower. Knowing too that this scene is near the campsite, spring and rock where Willard carved his name, we can imagine that the boys have brought the team here to drink before heading either past the Cinnabar Mine down to Denny or up over the Salmon divide toward Callahan.

156

Hiking down south from Mary Blaine Meadow, one passes the junction which promises a five mile hike southeast to Election Gap. That trail disappears many times before reaching such a destination, but it does pass by the living area for what was the Cinnabar Mine, both in the early 1900s and in later mining ventures. According to Grover Ladd, Peter Larcine only "scratched around" there, but in the 1930s it was the Hahns (or Hauns), who had been working at the Altoona, who dug two or three tunnels along a half-mile vein and "made grub out of it; it was during the hard times."[30] The trail toward Old Denny passes the Cinnabar Mine mercury retort. Cinnabar ore was heated until mercury was released as a gas, which was then cooled as it passed through a condenser and collected as liquid mercury or quicksilver.

Forty miles down to the mouth of New River, and west on U. S. Highway 299 to Willow Creek, travelers find a restaurant called Cinnabar Sam's. Its 19th century mining decor, Nellie Ladd photographs, old bottles, and an old bathtub celebrate the history of the Trinity Alps. Steve Paine, the owner, is so enthusiastic about local history that he created his own legendary character based on Peter Larcine, who really did own the Cinnabar Mine *(see pages 32 and 76)*, but has become a quite colorful imaginary character Steve calls "Cinnabar Sam." The legend is posted in the restaurant. When hikers stop by for a cool drink and a burger after a long hike out of the mountains, Steve is all ears, ready to hear the latest news from the mines and the ghost town of Old Denny.

Fig. 6-56. (V. Budig-Markin) The Cinnabar Mine mercury retort. 2001.

Fig. 6-57. (V. Budig-Markin) Steve Paine's restaurant, Cinnabar Sam's, Willow Creek. 2003.

Fig. 6-59. (V. Budig-Markin) The ten stamps
of the Ridgeway Mine stamp mill. 2001.

Fig. 6-58. (Nellie Ladd) The Ridgeway Mine power house
(left) and stamp mill (upper right). Below the stamp mill
is a huge ore debris pile from an adit above. 1910.

About two miles downhill of the Cinnabar Mine and just west of Marysville *(see area sketch, page 13)* was the Ridgeway Mine with its boiler-powered ten-stamp mill. This mill was unusual in its steam power and required substantial labor in the cutting of firewood to fuel the boilers. Most mines were operated by power from the local streams, running water wheels up to 33 feet in diameter and later Pelton wheels as small as 24 inches in diameter. Today, the ten half-ton stamps of the Ridgeway Mine lie unsupported by their original structure, which burned to the ground in a forest fire, with the giant boilers nearby.

Fig. 6-60. (V. Budig-Markin)
The Ridgeway Mine boilers. 2001.

At the Hunter Mine, less than a mile north of the Ridgeway, a pile of quartz about five feet high still remains unprocessed in front of the caved-in adit. Miners at the Hunter and the Ridgeway lived either next to the mines or in nearby Marysville.

Two of the last miners in the area were a Mr. Brink, "a German by name, a Dane by compulsion, and an American by choice,"[31] and his partner Andy Jacobsen. Brink died up at the head of Eagle Creek in 1933 and Jacobsen died in 1941. Grover Ladd talked about the problems carrying out Brink's body in the snow, and Grover and Bob Moore both tell about bringing out Jacobsen's body.[32]

The 2002 research team in the upper New River district included Grant Davis, the great-great grandson of pioneer miner Stephen Sherwood of the Sherwood Mine(s), as early as 1882 *(see pages 59, 60)*. Grant's great-great uncle Willis Sherwood died in a Fourth of July explosion in 1893 and his father Stephen died the next year, seemingly of grief. Another Sherwood son, Orin Parker Sherwood, was the Justice of the Peace in Old Denny (New River) in 1905 *(see pages 98-100)*. Grant was the first of his generation to make the long hike (about 13 miles) from today's Denny up 10 or 11 miles to Old Denny, then through Marysville and White Rock, to the Sherwood Mine. He visited the Ridgeway and Hunter mines, inspecting the unprocessed quartz ore at the Hunter for traces of gold. Researchers found that the width of the quartz veins measured about nine inches.

Fig. 6-61. (V. Budig-Markin) Quartz ore near caved-in adit at the Hunter Mine. 2002.

Fig. 6-62. (V. Budig-Markin) Grant Davis inspects a quartz ore sample at the Hunter Mine. 2002.

159

Fig. 6-63. (V. Budig-Markin) Grant Davis contemplates two graves in White Rock. 2002.

White Rock and Old Denny had the two cemeteries in the upper New River mining district. Grant Davis stopped at a double grave in the White Rock cemetery (Fig. 6-63) to meditate on the past and imagine that these were the graves of family members Stephen and Willis Sherwood. The two-story hotel at the left of Fig. 6-64 has disappeared with the Brizard store, the post office, the saloons, the cabins, the miners, their families and White Rock's celebrated musicians.

Fig. 6-64. (Nellie Ladd) White Rock. 1896. Original print 1 7/8" x 1 7/16" plus mat.

About a half mile north, beyond White Rock, one crosses Sherwood Creek and turns downstream and west to approach the Sherwood Mine. The two stamps of the mill lie under a burned timber at the stamp mill site. The fine screen of the ore dump is visible under a carriage spring lying across one of the fallen stamps (Fig. 6-65). Hot and thirsty, Grant goes down from the stamp mill to get water (Fig. 6-66) from Sherwood Creek. The fine sandy dirt behind him suggests that the mine may also have had an arrastra here by the creek.

Fig. 6-65. (V. Budig-Markin) Stamp mill detail, Sherwood Mine. 2002. *(See page 98, Fig. 4-4.)*

Color photos © Valerie Budig-Markin

Fig. 6-66. (V. Budig-Markin) Grant Davis gets water from Sherwood Creek. 2002.

Over the years since 1999, the researchers have passed the baton and shared measurements, sketches, photos and site records. Elaine Sundahl wrote the site reports for Old Denny and the Ridgeway Mine. Gay Berrien wrote the site record for White Rock and is continuing site record preparation, along with James Barnes, Bureau of Land Management archeologist.

Bill Sundahl, longtime student of nature and cheerful sage of the crew, is one of the steady core reseachers. Susanne Rinne, Professor of French, English and German, has come from Germany for three summers to participate in the cultural history research.

Fig. 6-67 (Valerie Budig-Markin) (Rear L-R) **Bill Sundahl, Susanne Rinne, Ed Holland, Gay Berrien, John Palmquist;** (front) **Wayne Moss, Pat Craig. 2001.**

Ed Holland, retired auditor of the California State Employment offices in Eureka, cooks the send-off meal each year and cooks up a storm during the week of research. He and Gay Berrien contribute their trailhead cabin (in new Denny), the shopping and most of the cost of the supplies and mule train for Old Denny base camp. Gay shares past documentation, reference materials, and stories from the Weaverville *Trinity Journal* by the evening campfire in years when the fire danger is not too extreme. John Palmquist is a faithful participant and an indefatigable bushwacker and site scout. Wayne Moss, author of the *Trinity Alps Companion* and retired vice-superintendent of schools in Weaverville, has many a tale to tell about the local characters, animals and wilderness trails. Unpictured storytellers include Howard May and Bob Maloney.

Pat Craig walks those eleven miles up to Old Denny year after year with infinite cheerfulness and perseverance and sets up the kitchen at base camp before heading up further to measure and record mine and town sites with the others. Crews of up to 12 share both solidarity and research.

Fig. 6-68. (VBM) Ed Holland serves pancakes to John Palmquist at dawn. 2003.

Fig. 6-69. (VBM) (L-R) Rob Robinson, Stephanie Low, Bill Sundahl at the Boomer stamp mill. 2003.

Fig. 6-70. (V. Budig-Markin) (Rear L-R) **Randy Steinbeck** (ready for Nellie Ladd photo re-enactment), **Leon Cody, Darlene Cody, Ed Holland, Rob Robinson, John Palmquist, Bill Sundahl.** (Front L-R) **Stephanie Low, Gay Berrien, Barbara Bergstrom, Valerie Budig-Markin. Boomer sawmill site. 2003.**

Fig. 6-71. (VBM) Barbara Bergstrom picks an onion-like plant she once used for soup. Boomer pond. 2003.

Fig. 6-72. (VBM) Susanne Rinne and Ron Craig explore ruins of the Excelsior stamp mill. 2001.

Fig. 6-73. (VBM) Bill Sundahl tells a ghost story while John Palmquist and Barbara Bergstrom listen. 2003.

162

June 2003 expedition photos
courtesy of Rob Robinson.

163

John Palmquist participates every year in the expeditions up New River to town and mine sites. He also provides suggestions and encourages Gay Berrien in her quest for funding for Old Denny research. Donations are accepted by the Trinity County Historical Society, Box 333, Weaverville, CA, 96093.

Fig. 6-74. (V. Budig-Markin) John Palmquist measures bear paw prints next to those of mountain lions in the mud at the site of Lake City, on Pony Creek. 2001.

Fig. 6-75. (Rebekah Burgess) Peter Palmquist, founder and curator, Women in Photography International Archive. 1979.

Peter Palmquist, John's brother, first published a small book with Nellie Ladd photographs titled, *Nellie Ladd: Photographs of Old Denny, California 1895-1920.*[33] He was Gay Berrien's photographic consultant for the traveling Nellie Ladd photograph exhibit, shown in seven cities in California and Nevada maintained by the Trinity County Historical Society. Peter Palmquist, staff photographer for 28 years until 1989 at Humboldt State University in Arcata, CA, is considered one of the foremost photo-historians of the 20th century. His principal interests were the American West, California, Humboldt County before 1950, and women photographers worldwide. He published over 60 books, curated scores of exhibitions and delivered hundreds of lectures. He was also the founder of the Women in Photography International Archive. His entire archive was transferred to the Beinecke Library at Yale University. A professional photographer for 50 years, he recorded events in Paris for the U. S. Army with the Supreme Headquarters Allied Powers Europe (SHAPE). In Humboldt County, he served on the Board of Directors of the Humboldt Arts Council, the Clarke Memorial Museum, and the Humboldt County Historical Society.[34] He was a key figure in the support of the preservation and dissemination of Nellie Ladd's photography. He also hiked and loved the Trinity Alps where she lived, and he took AFS foreign exchange students for hikes in the Trinity Alps with his brother John. Peter was killed by a hit-and-run driver in Emeryville, California, in January, 2003.

NOTES

CHAPTER VI

1. Frank Wallen, Jr., conversation with the author January, 2000; Gay Holland Berrien, "The Wallen Ranch and the Irving Family of Hawkins Creek," *Trinity 1996,* p. 36.

2. Wallen, January, 2000.

3. Wallen, January, 2000.

4. Berrien, *Trinity 1996,* p. 43, 48, 49; Wallen, January, 2000..

5. Grover Ladd, Interview 1965 by Gay Holland.

6. Gay Berrien, conversations 2000, 2001.

7. Robert "Bob" McGregor Moore, telephone interview July 8, 2003.

8. Grover Ladd, interview 1965 by Gay Holland.

9. Michael and Catherine Moore, conversation July 1, 2003. Michael's three sisters are Linda, who lives in Choctaw, OK; Susie, in Medford, OR; and Patty, in Portland, OR.

10. Grover's collie was known as "the coyote-eating collie," according to Gay Berrien. The collie and Bobbie Moore became good friends.

11. Gay Berrien, e-mail correspondence January, 2003.

12. Gay Berrien, conversation July, 2000.

13. Michael Moore remembered Grover's cherries and the trip to Denny to attend Clara's funeral in 1952. That was the day Grover made Michael a sluice box and took him panning for gold. Conversation with the author, July 1, 2003.

14. Gay Berrien, conversations 2000-2003.

15. Gay Berrien, conversation April, 2003.

16. Barbara Bergstrom, conversations June, 2003.

17. Smokey Bergstrom, conversation June 2002.18. Smokey and Barbara Bergstrom, conversations 2002, 2003.

19. Darlene Cody and Barbara Bergstrom, conversation with the author March, 2003.

20. Both women are wonderful storytellers and welcomed in the author like Nellie Ladd or Kate Irving must have done in their time for curious travelers to the mountains.

21. Stories on this page by Barbara Bergstrom and Darlene Cody, mostly from their conversation with the author in March, 2003

22. In the summer of 2003, Leon and Darlene Cody, their son Frank and about a dozen other young adults came up to the Tough Nut to dig out the Cody cabin from three to eight feet of rocks and earth left in and around their cabin by a snowslide in the winter of 2001-2002. Hard work liberated the cabin and provided material for a front yard, where only a mountain slope had existed before. The slide was reminiscent of the 1890 snowslide that killed John Lewis and almost killed Frank Ladd at the Mountain Boomer Mine less than 1/2 mile away.

23. Grover Ladd, interview 1965 by Gay Holland.

24. The cookhouse and its kitchen have left only traces of their frame construction and a water line coming down to them from the Boomer Pond a mile uphill. Once there was also an ice house to the left (north) of the lower kitchen building in Fig. 6-27. Partly buried in the hillside, according to Grover Ladd, it protected winter ice for summer use with walls filled with sawdust three feet thick. Grover Ladd, 1965.

Randy Steinbeck, present-day co-owner of the Tough Nut Mine and owner of the Bergstrom cabin, has hiked around the area for decades and is familiar with the Boomer, the Tough Nut and the abandoned mine sites around them. He, too, is a generous host and a good storyteller. He hiked with the June 2003 research group and appears in Figs. 6-28, 6-30, 6-33, 6-34, 6-70 and on page 163 in a Rob Robinson photograph of the Boomer stamp mill site.

25. This modern-day photograph reveals what the unknown man in Fig. 6-29 saw when zeroing in his rifle in about 1905. The view to the northwest is the hillside of the Tough Nut Mine on the right and, in the center, the Slide Creek drainage in the direction of Old Denny.

26. Randy Steinbeck, conversation June, 2003.

27. The New River research crew has four main goals:
  1) to record the historic sites of the Old Denny Historic District, both from field and archival research;
  2) to share this information with the public through the Trinity County Historical Society;
  3) to generally increase awareness and appreciation for northwestern Trinity County's history; and
  4) to educate the public that it is illegal and unethical to pick up artifacts and relics on public lands, such as in the upper New River.
  The Antiquities Act of 1906 made it illegal to disturb or remove artifacts, but the Act was not widely publicized or enforced in the Trinity Alps area.
  The Archeological Resources Protection Act of 1979 emphasized and strengthened the protection of historic and prehistoric artifacts and features, and makes it a felony in many instances to disturb or remove these objects.
  Donations to assist in the volunteer research of Old Denny and the upper New River mining district may be sent to the Trinity County Historical Society, Post Office Box 333, Weaverville, CA 96093.

28. Trinity County Historical Society, Post Office Box 333, Weaverville, CA 96093.

29. Randy Steinbeck told the author, in June of 2003, how to find this six-foot rock on the west side of Mary Blaine Meadow, near a spring and a campsite. See page 156.

30. Grover Ladd, interview 1965 by Gay Holland.

31. Quoted by Grover Ladd in 1965 interview by Gay Holland.

32. Grover Ladd, interview 1965 by Gay Holland; Bob Moore, telephone interview by the author, August 2003.

33. This 52-page book includes an introductory essay about Nellie Ladd and 40 of her photographs. It is available through the Trinity County Historical Society (see note 28).

34. *Peter E. Palmquist, 1936-2003*, memorial booklet, page 4, printed by Eureka Printing, Eureka, CA.

Photographs and Illustrations

The following index lists the sources of many Nellie Ladd photographs. The Trinity County Historical Society may be contacted in writing about the Nellie Ladd Collection at P. O. Box 333, Weaverville, CA 96093. Information regarding the R. S. Holland Collection may be obtained by contacting Gay Berrien, P. O. Box 669, Big Bar, CA 96010.

Trinity County Historical Society & R. S. Holland Collection Catalogue Numbers

Page	Fig. No.	Ladd Coll. Cat.No.	Holland Coll. Cat. No.	Other
Cover		6.11		
Title		1.4		
1		4.24		
4	1 2	22.4		
5	1 4	25.15		
8	1 7	2.28		
9	1 8			X
10	1 9			X
11	1 10			X
13	1 12	25.20		
14	1 13			X
15	1 13	4.24		
17	1 18	18.26		
18	1 19	6.12		
19	1 20	24.3		
20	1 21			X
21	1 22			X
24	1 25	18.10		
25	1 27			X
26	1 28		rsh.46	
26	1 29		rsh.46	
28	1 30	25.26		
28	1 31	4.33		
29	1 32	18.24		
30	1 33	6.21		
32	1 34			X
33	1 35	17.21		
37		20.15		
39	2 4	20.15		
39	2 5			X
40	2 6	20.17		
40	2 7	4.28		
41	2 8	9.1		
42	2 9			X
43	2 10			X
44	2 11	25.2		
45	2 12			X
46	2 13	2.30		
47	2 14	1.4		
48	2 15	6.24		
49	2 16	9.22		
50	2 17	17.24/20.23		
51	2 18	20.12		
52	2 19	18.16		
53	2 20	8.35		
54	2 21			X
55	2 22	6.9		
56	2 23			X
57	2 24	25.13		
61	3 2			X
63	3 3	18.17		
65	3 4	6.27		
67	3 6	4.17	rsh.10	
68	3 7			X
69	3 8	18.15		
71	3 10		rsh.38	
72	3 11			X
73	3 12		rsh.--	
74	3 13	6.26		
75	3 14	18.5		
77	3 15		rsh.7	X
78	3 16			X
79	3 17	18.18	rsh.58	
80	3 18	11.22		
81	3 19	11.29		
82	3 20	14.7		
83	3 21	19.5		
84	3 22			X
85	3 23	2.9		
86	3 24		rsh.39	
87	3 25			X
88	3 26			X
89	3 27	17.26		
93				X
94	4 1	8.25		
95	4 2			X
97	4 3	25.14	rsh.48	
99	4 6	6.4/6.33		
100	4 7		rsh.44	
102	4 9	12.18		
103	4 10		rsh.66	
104	4 11	18.14		
105	4 12	18.9	rsh.10	
106	4 13			X
107	4 14	6.30		
107	4 15	6.17		
108	4 17			X
108	4 18			X
108	4 19	18.9	rsh.10	
109	4 20	2.27		
110	4 22	6.29		

Page	Fig. No.	Ladd Coll. Cat.No.	Holland Coll. Cat. No.	Other
111	4 23	6.28		
111	4 24			X
112	4 25	17.7		
113	4 26		rsh.50	X
114	4 27	6.34		
115	4 28	19.27		
116	4 29	4.33		
116	4 30			X
117	4 31	8.1		
118	4 32	6.1		
119	2 18	20.12		
119	4 12	18.9		
119	4 33	20.12		
119	4 34	18.9		
121	4-36			X
127	5 2	1.6/17.14		
128	5 3	1.8		
129	5 4	1.7	rsh.42	
130	5 5	1.18/17.3		
131	5 6	25.5		
132	5 7	9.6		
133	5 8	24.14		
134	5 9	24.12		
135	5 10	20.25		
136	5 11	16.17		
137	5 12	24.15		
141	6 4	13.27		
141	5 10	20.25		
148	6 25			X (see p. 72)
149	6 27			X
149	6 29	18.5		
150	6 32			X
151	6 35	4.24		
152	6 39	2.27		
153	6 42	1.6/17.14		
153	6 44	6.9		
154	6 47			X
154	6 48	25.14	rsh.48	
156	6 54	1.4		
158	6 58		rsh.7	X
160	6 64	8.11		

Digitized prints of historic photographs. Original photography and considerable deterioration of some photographs, negatives and glass slides made scanning and touch-up processes difficult. In digital reproduction, both Chromogenics Photography and the author attempted to maintain a balance between authenticity and quality of the resulting prints. Prints produced by Chromogenics appear on the cover, title page and pages 1, 4, 5, 8-11, 13-15, 17-19, 21, 24, 28 (Fig. 1-30), 30, 32, 37, 39-42, 44, 46-51, 53-55, 57, 63, 65, 68, 71, 72, 74-76, 79-83, 85-88, 95, 97, 99, 104, 107, 109, 111-115, 117, 118 and 189. Other digitized work by the author.

Modern photographs. The following photographs by the author are copyrighted: Figs. 6-2, 6-3, photos p. 144, Figs. 6-15, 6-16, 6-24, 6-26, 6-28, 6-30, 6-33, 6-36, 6-37, 6-38, 6-49, 6-53, 6-59, 6-60, 6-63, 6-65, 6-66. Photographs by Rob Robinson, including all photographs on p. 163 plus Figs. 6-51 and 6-52, may only be used or reprinted by written permission from the photographer. Photograph of the author on the back cover of the book is by Susanne Rinne. All other individual photographs by photographers as noted; modern color photographs used with permission as noted.

Photograph captions: names in parentheses are those of the respective photographers. Numbering of photographs hereafter refers to chapter and photographs in each chapter.

Cover photograph by Nellie Ladd, self-titled: "Coming Down," photograph taken at Robber's Roost, c. 1915.

Title page photograph by Nellie Ladd: "Grover, Willard Ladd guide the mule train across Mary Blaine Meadow, Pony Buttes backdrop," c. 1907.

Copyrighted illustrations by the author include area sketch, p. 3; salamander, dogbane, p. 4; area sketch, p. 13; tin pitcher, china logo, bottle, p. 16; glass plate camera, family camera, p. 38; iron candleholder, p. 64.

APPENDIX A: 1872-1896 New River Precinct Voters

NEW RIVER VOTERS, 1872-1896

Name	Born	Occupation	Precinct	Earliest Reg. Date	Name	Born	Occupation	Precinct	Earliest Reg. Date
Adams, Alfred	MS	Miner	Hoboken	8/20/1873	Clinton, William Howard	NY		New River	10/10/1890
Anderson, Richard K.	MS		New River	7/23/1884	Coeur, Alexander	France		New River	5/21/1884
Bagley, Evan Thomas	PA	Miner	New River	9/21/1888	Colgrove, Francis	NY	Miner	New River	9/23/1892
Bailey, William	Canada	Farmer	Hoboken	10/22/1892	Davis, Francis James	Canada	Miner	New River	6/24/1879
Baker, Edward	Canada		New River	7/23/1884	Dean, George	NH	Miner	New River	9/21/1886
Baker, Thomas J.	IL		New River	8/22/1884	Dennis, Christopher Cummins	NJ		New River	10/2/1886
Barron, John M.	KY	Blacksmith	New River	4/2/1877	Dickhoff, John Henry	Germany		New River	8/14/1884
Barron, Joseph	IN	Miner	New River	4/2/1877	Diggins, John	IL	Miner	New River	4/2/1877
Black, Peter Patterson	MO		New River	7/23/1884	Donald, William J.	ME	Miner	New River	9/30/1880
Block, Hans A.	Sweden		New River	4/11/1884	Duncan, James W.	IN	Builder	Hoboken	9/7/1880
Boles, John	NY	Miner	Hoboken	8/29/1877	Dunlap, Valentine	PA	Miner	Hoboken	10/22/1892
Bontecou, Edward	NY	Miner	New River	11/13/1866	Dyer, George	CA		Hoboken	10/16/1890
Bowerman, Harvey	Canada		New River	6/15/1886	Dyer, Orrington S.	ME	Miner	New River	9/1/1866
Boyd, Alexander	NJ	Miner	New River	9/26/1892	Ellis, Charles Starr	MA	Clerk	New River	8/5/1896
Boyle, Henry	OH	Miner	New River	10/7/1882	Farnham, Nason T.	ME	Shipwright	Hoboken	9/9/1880
Boynton, William Nelson	VT		New River	6/15/1886	Ferguson, Peter Shannon	IN	Miner	Hoboken	8/10/1896
Braw, Joseph Francis	Portugal	Miner	New River	7/8/1879	Francis, Joseph M.	France	Merchant	New River	6/25/1880
Breedlove, John J.	KY	Miner	New River	6/11/1867	Franks, George	CA		New River	10/2/1884
Brooks, Smith Baldwin	OH	Miner	New River	7/17/1884	Franzen, James Christian	Prussia		New River	9/19/1888
Brown, Lemuel	NC	Farmer	Pony Creek	7/3/1867	Fulmore, Archibald G.	Nova Scotia	Miner	New River	6/29/1888
Buckley, Thomas	England	Miner	New River	8/9/1869	Gabriel, George William	OH	Clerk	Hoboken	10/3/1892
Cain, Thomas	PA	Miner	New River	8/22/1876	Garlow, Frank Pratt	OH		New River	9/14/1888
Campbell, Thomas Gustave	KY		New River	7/30/1884	Garrett, William	OH		New River	6/15/1886
Caraway, Virgil	VA	Merchant	New River	3/18/1867	Geyer, Charles H.	Germany	Miner	New River	7/18/1877
Carothes, Manuel	Western Isls		New River	8/14/1884	Gray, David Baskins	PA	Miner	New River	11/13/1866
Carroll, Benjamin Franklin	TN	Woodsman	New River	10/18/1894	Guillaume, Phillip	Prussia	Miner	New River	6/11/1867
Carson, Sylvester D.	ME	Miner	New River	9/9/1880	Gulick, James Henry	NJ	Miner	New River	9/9/1880
Christopher, James Russell	TN		New River	6/15/1886	Gutzen, Gustave	Russia		New River	7/10/1886
Clark, Abner Leland	ME	Miner	New River	6/16/1888	Gwine, William	KY	Miner	New River	8/9/1869
Clement, Oliver C.	IL		New River	7/24/1884	Hackelman, John	IN	Miner	Hoboken	8/23/1875
Clement, William Henry	IA	Miner	New River	8/31/1892	Hammill, George Washington	OH		New River	7/23/1884

NEW RIVER VOTERS, 1872-1896 (cont'd.)

Name	Born	Occupation	Precinct	Earliest Reg. Date	Name	Born	Occupation	Precinct	Earliest Reg. Date
Haney, James Sarsfield	New Bruns.		New River	5/25/1888	Maloney, William	Ireland		New River	5/25/1888
Hanson, Charles	Norway	Miner	New River	6/29/1888	Mann, William Franklin	KS	Miner	New River	10/10/1894
Hanson, John	Denmark	Woodsman	New River	7/9/1896	Markham, Thomas Bartholom	Ireland	Miner	New River	10/19/1892
Hanson, John F.G.	Norway		Hoboken	10/1/1886	Martin, Frank	Azore Isls.	Miner	New River	8/15/1871
Hardy, Robert	PA	Miner	Hoboken	8/24/1877	Maxwell, Azariah Willard	New Bruns.		New River	9/27/1886
Harrison, John	OH		New River	7/24/1884	McAtee, Charles Sidney	IA	Miner	Hoboken	9/12/1892
Hely, Gorges Vicar	Ireland	Miner	New River	9/30/1880	McDonald, James McD	MS	Miner	New River	6/24/1879
Hennessey, John Patrick	CA	Miner	New River	6/29/1888	McDonald, Murdock Corneliu:	MI	Millwright	Hoboken	10/17/1894
Herrick, Isaiah Brown	ME		New River	6/15/1886	McDowell, William Rufus	OH		New River	10/4/1890
Herschberger, Jacob S.	PA	Miner	New River	4/2/1877	McKeene, Anciel Lewis	ME	Miner	Hoboken	8/4/1869
Holz, Peter Paul	France	Miner	Hoboken	7/17/1896	McLeod, John	Nova Scotia		New River	9/29/1890
Huestis, George Washington	NJ		New River	7/24/1884	McLeod, William	Pr.Edw Is.	Miner	Hoboken	7/21/1896
Huestis, Theodore F.	IA		New River	7/23/1884	Miles, William	PA	Miner	New River	9/9/1880
Huff, Charles E.	ME	Miner	New River	10/7/1882	Miller, George A.	WI	Carpenter	Hoboken	9/9/1880
Hussey, Edwin H.	ME		New River	6/15/1886	Miller, John	Sweden	Miner	New River	9/20/1892
Irving, George Jackson	New Bruns.	Miner	New River	8/31/1892	Miller, John Edward	CA	Miner	New River	10/4/1890
Jillson, William Oliver	NY		New River	10/2/1884	Mills, Martin Luther	CA		New River	6/15/1886
Keach, John T.	KY	Miner	New River	11/13/1866	Mills, William	PA	Miner	New River	7/24/1884
Kerby, Francis M.	NC	Miner	New River	8/9/1880	Morris, Alonzo P.	NY	Seaman	Hoboken	8/24/1877
Kinkead, James Irvin	KY		New River	5/25/1888	Mosher, Aaron	PA		New River	8/25/1888
Ladd, Frank James	ME	Miner	New River	8/14/1884	Mowers, George	Scotland	Miner	New River	6/24/1879
Laederich, Henry Emil	CA		New River	10/4/1890	Mullane, James	Ireland	Butcher	North Fork	10/2/1868
Lamberson, Daniel Perry	MI	Miner	New River	7/29/1896	Mullane, Thomas Keely	CA	Miner	New River	9/12/1892
Larcine, Peter	France	Hotelkeeper	New River	10/4/1890	Murphy, James	Ireland	Laborer	New River	9/30/1880
Leas, John Carrington	MN	Miner	New River	6/16/1886	Murphy, John Bernard	Ireland	Miner	Hoboken	10/3/1892
Leonard, Nelson	OH	Merchant	Hoboken	6/9/1880	Mylott, Andrew E.	Ireland		New River	3/26/1886
Levegne, Charles	Canada		New River	10/10/1890	Newsome, Benjamin	NY		New River	6/15/1886
Lundberg, Alfred	Prussia	Miner	New River	9/20/1892	Newton, James	Scotland		New River	9/11/1888
Lupton, George	NE	Miner	Hoboken	8/5/1896	Nichols, William John	WI	Miner	Hoboken	10/22/1892
Lupton, William	CA	Laborer	Hoboken	9/9/1880	Nicholson, Thomas Moore	IN	Miner	New River	7/10/1886
Main, Albert	NY	Miner	New River	9/30/1880	Noble, Frank	CA	Miner	Hoboken	8/5/1896

NEW RIVER VOTERS, 1872-1896   (cont'd.)

Name	Born	Occupation	Precinct	Earliest Reg. Date	Name	Born	Occupation	Precinct	Earliest Reg. Date
Noble, Joseph	CA	Hatter	Hoboken	10/17/1894	Sherwood, Stephen	PA	Blacksmith	New River	6/24/1879
Noble, Stephen	ME	Miner	New River	8/14/1869	Shook, Hiram Reynold		Miner	Hoboken	10/3/1892
Noble, William	CA		New River	9/21/1888	Short, George Washington	CA		New River	10/2/1886
Noble, William	CA	Miner	Hoboken	10/3/1892	Shuford, John William	CA		New River	6/15/1886
Oman, Olaf Emil	Denmark	Miner	New River	6/24/1879	Silva, Antone	Western Isls	Miner	New River	6/15/1880
O'Neil, Stephen	WI		New River	6/2/1888	Sinclair, James Duncan	Canada		New River	7/10/1886
Osgood, Alva	CA		New River	6/29/1888	Singer, Richard S.	PA		New River	10/4/1884
Osgood, Rufus E.	ME	Mechanic	New River	9/9/1880	Smith, Alfred W.	CA	Painter	Hoboken	9/9/ 1880
Palmer, Elbridge F.	NY	Foreman	New River	8/23/1880	Smith, Henry	Germany		New River	10/1/1886
Palmer, Robert H.	NY	Engineer	Hoboken	9/9/1880	Smith, Jerry	PA		New River	4/11/1884
Patterson, James Henry	CA	Farmer	Hoboken	8/5/1896	Soule, Hannibal Scott	VT		New River	9/21/1886
Patterson, Moses	NY	Farmer	New River	11/13/1866	Stephenson, Millard Fillmore	IL		Hoboken	10/3/1890
Penwell, Benjamin	CA	Miner	Hoboken	8/5/1896	Stoody, David McConnell	OH	Miner	New River	9/2/1886
Phares, Henry Clifford	IA		New River	8/18/1888	Stout, Frank S.	MN	Miner	Hoboken	8/8/1896
Price, Alonzo Stephen	England	Stone cutter	New River	6/24/1879	Stover, Henry	Germany		New River	9/15/1884
Quimby, Charles	CA		New River	7/24/1884	Stuhr, Christian	Germany	Miner	New River	4/2/1877
Quimby, Cyrus W.	ME	Farmer	New River	8/9/1867	Sullivan, George J.	NY		New River	10/2/1884
Richardson, Charles H.	MA	Blacksmith	New River	7/25/1868	Taylor, Stephen F.	OH	Contractor	Hoboken	9/9/1880
Richot, A.D.	Canada		New River	7/23/1884	Thomas, Benjamin F.	CA	Trader	Hoboken	8/24/1877
Roberts, Manuel	Portugal		New River	5/26/1885	Thomas, Robert Jr.	CA		New River	9/10/1884
Roff, George	Canada		New River	6/15/1886	Thomas, Robert Lewis	VA	Farmer	New River	9/14/1866
Rowan, Michael	Ireland	Miner	New River	10/30/1880	Thomas, Watham L.	NY	Engineer	Hoboken	8/31/1877
Rozzan, Frank	Italy	Miner	New River	10/19/1892	Thompson, John Mitchell	VA		New River	10/2/1886
Savor, Paul	ME	Miner	New River	7/5/1879	Thynge, John	MA		New River	6/29/1888
Sayre, Tehil Halsey	NY		New River	10/2/1884	Trimmer, William W.	UT		New River	6/15/1886
Scott, Joseph Preston	IA	Miner	Hoboken	6/20/1896	Van Male, John James	Holland		Coeur	6/15/1888
Scott, Sylvester David	OH	Miner	New River	6/15/1886	Vaughn, William Manley	ME		New River	8/25/1888
Sharber, John	Germany		New River	7/24/1884	Vetore, John	Portugal	Miner	New River	6/20/1877
Sheehy, John	PA		New River	10/2/1884	Wagner, Frederick	IN	Miner	New River	4/2/1877
Sheffield, Eliazer E.	OH		New River	9/21/1886	Walker, George W.	IL	Farmer	New River	8/21/1880
Sherwood, Oren P.	IL		New River	6/15/1886	Wall, Joseph	PA	Laborer	New River	6/30/1879

NEW RIVER VOTERS, 1872-1896   (cont'd.)

Name	Born	Occupation	Precinct	Earliest Reg. Date
Washington, Orrin	VA		Hoboken	10/1/1886
Watkins, Benjamin Franklin			Hoboken	7/24/1884
Wetsel, Willis Austin	NY	Miner	Hoboken	7/20/1896
Whitney, William	ME	Mason	Hoboken	8/29/1877
Wilkinson, Robert	Ireland	Miner	Hoboken	10/3/1892
Willburn, Frederick P.	TX	Laborer	Hoboken	9/23/1880
Williams, Charles G.	VT		New River	6/15/1886
Williams, William	TN	Miner	New River	11/13/1866
Wills, Richard W.	VA		New River	10/2/1884
Wyman, Joseph Fraswar	Luxembourg	Miner	Hoboken	7/29/1896
Yocum, Albert Eugene	CA	Miner	New River	10/4/1894
Yocum, Geo. Wash. Brush	KY	Miner	New River	8/31/1892
Zane, Jeremiah Franklin	CA		New River	7/10/1886
Zeigler, Isaiah	OH		New River	9/27/1886

Research and information from the Trinity County Great Register by Gay Berrien, 2003.

APPENDIX B: 1900 Census for New River Township

The following five-page document is from the Twelfth Census of the United States, State of California, Trinity County, New River Township. The people are listed in the sequence they were recorded, as Gay Berrien notes, from the White Rock area and upper New River (about 40 residents) down New River (30 more residents), and the rest in Hawkins Bar, Burnt Ranch, and Salyer, all on the Trinity River. Part of a page of the actual census report, copied and pieced together from microfilm from the California State Library, is printed below, showing the meticulously written original record of the information "Enumerated by me (Albert Yocum) on the 7th day of June, 1900."

Of note in the census regarding the Ladds, **Ellen (Nellie) E. Ladd**'s birth month and year, Dec., 1860, are different than various dates listed in other sources. This census also indicates she had a third child who died, a fact mentioned nowhere else in local texts. This probably means that she had a child born and died during her first marriage to Mr. Graham, a marriage only surmised, given her second family name of Graham when she married Frank Ladd in 1886. We also know Nellie was raised in Massachusetts but not born there, as indicated in the census. Perhaps someone else gave Bert Yocum the Ladd household information in Nellie's absence. As for **Frank Ladd**, his occupation is listed as "Grocer," surprising given his continuing gold mine operations, even after buying the store, around 1894. We also note two boarders at the Ladds, a student and the schoolteacher at the time.

The census includes native Americans like **Jim Chesbrow (Chesbro)** in the main listing, and again in two sections dedicated to the **"Indian Population."** Interestingly enough, Jim Chesbro, the mail carrier *(see page 5)*, could read but not write, according to the census data. The special section at the end includes categories such as whether the person, if "Indian," is living in polygamy; the year the person obtained U. S. citizenship; and if that citizenship was obtained by allotment or not. Finally, the census asks whether the person's dwelling is fixed or movable. While "white" men are sometimes listed as living in tents, no native American is so listed.

TWELFTH CENSUS OF THE UNITED STATES 1900
CALIFORNIA, TRINITY COUNTY, NEW RIVER TOWNSHIP

	NAME	RELATION	COLOR RACE	SEX	D.O.B. MO,YR	AGE	S,M, W,D	YRS MAR	MOTH # CH.	# CH. Living	BIRTH PLACE THIS PERSON	BIRTH PLACE FATHER	BIRTH PLACE MOTHER	OCCUPATION	READ	WRITE	SPEAK ENGL	OWN/ RENT
1	McDowell, Edwin	Head	W	M	May, 1843	57	S				Ohio	Ireland	Maryland	Miner (Qtz.)	yes	yes	yes	Own
2	_____ William R.	Brother	W	M	Jan, 1849	51	S				Ohio	Ireland	Maryland	Miner (Qtz.)	yes	yes	yes	
3	Horner, Oscar	Head	W	M	Jan, 1838	62	S				Vermont	Ireland	Vermont	Miner (Qtz.)	yes	yes	yes	
4	Colby, John	Head	W	M	Jan, 18343	57	M	7			Maine	Maine	Maine	Carpenter	yes	yes	yes	
5	Samberson, Daniel	Head	W	M	Sept, 1846	53	S				Michigan	Pennsylvania	New York	Miner (Qtz.)	yes	yes	yes	Own
6	Sherwood, Oren P.	Head	W	M	Apr, 1840	60	S				Illinois	Pennsylvania	Vermont	Miner (Qtz.)	yes	yes,yes		Own
7	Perkins, Thomas	Head	W	M	June, 1840	60	S				Ireland 1854Na	Ireland	Ireland	Miner (Qtz.)	yes	yes	yes	Rent
8	Healy, George V.	Head	W	M	Jan, 1838	62	S				Ireland 1840Na	Ireland	Ireland	Miner (Qtz.)	yes	yes	yes	Own
9	Blais, Eli	Head	W	M	Jan, 1852	48	M	17			Vermont	Canada (Fr.)	Canada (Fr.)	Miner (Qtz.)	yes	yes	yes	Rent
10	Gulick, James H.	Head	W	M	Jan, 1844	56	S				New Jersey	New Jersey	New Jersey	Miner (Qtz.)	yes	yes	yes	Own
11	Bartlett, John H.	Head	W	M	Sept, 1865	34	M	9			California	New Hampshire	Ireland	Mine Superint.	yes	yes	yes	Rent
12	_____ Mary	Wife	W	F	Oct, 1871	28	M	9	1	1	California	England	Ohio		yes	yes	yes	
13	_____ Alice	Daughter	W	F	Oct, 1891	8	S				California	California	California	At School	yes	yes		
14	Larcine, Peter O.	Head	W	M	Feb, 1833	67	M	18			Florida	France	France	Hotel	yes	yes	yes	Own
15	_____ Celina	Wife	W	F	Jan, 1844	56	M	18	1	1	Missouri	So. Carolina	Kentucky		yes	yes	yes	
16	_____ Mary B.	Daughter	W	F	Aug, 1883	16	S				California	Florida	Missouri	At School	yes	yes	yes	
17	Noble, Martha	Boarder	M,I 1/2	F	Feb, 1887	13	S				California	California	California	At School	yes	yes	yes	
18	Ramutt, Christopher	Boarder	W	M	Oct, 1863	36	S				Wisconsin	Norway	Norway	Miner (Qtz.)	yes	yes	yes	
19	Nelson, Elmir (?)	Head	W	M	Aug, 1875	24	S				Utah	Sweden	Sweden	Miner (Qtz.)	yes	yes	yes	Rent
20	_____ Edward O.	Brother	W	M	Oct, 1879	20	S				Utah	Sweden	Sweden	Miner (Qtz.)	yes	yes	yes	
21	_____ Clara M.	Sister	W	F	Nov, 1881	18	S				Utah	Sweden	Sweden		yes	yes	yes	
22	_____ Rudolph	Brother	W	M	Dec, 1883	16	S				Utah	Sweden	Sweden	At School	yes	yes	yes	
23	_____ May I. (?)	Sister	W	F	May, 1887	13	S				Utah	Sweden	Sweden	At School	yes	yes	yes	
24	Yocum, George W. B	Head	W	M	Aug, 1828	71	D				Kentucky	Kentucky	Kentucky		yes	yes	yes	Own
25	_____ Albert E.	Son	W	M	Feb, 1856	44	S				California	Kentucky	Ohio	Amalgamation	yes	yes	yes	
26	Ladd, Frank J. (?)	Head	W	M	Jan, 1852	48	M	13			Maine	Maine	Maine	Grocer	yes	yes	yes	Own
27	_____ Ellen E.	Wife	W	F	Dec, 1860	39	M	13	3	2	Massachusetts	Ireland	France		yes	yes	yes	
28	_____ Grover H.	Son	W	M	July, 1887	12	S				California	Maine	Massachusetts	At School	yes	yes	yes	
29	_____ Willard W.	Son	W	M	Jan, 1889	11	S				California	Maine	Massachusetts	At School	yes	yes	yes	
30	Coady, Bessie C.	Boarder	W	F	Mar, 1876	24	S				California	Ireland	Ireland	Teacher(school)	yes	yes	yes	
31	Noble, Laura	Boarder	M,I 1/2	F	Sept, 1883	16	S				California	Maine	California	At School	yes	yes	yes	
32	Martin, John, Jr. (?)	Head	W	M	Novv, 1859	40	S				Missouri	Kentucky	Tennessee	Miner (Qtz.)	yes	yes	yes	Rent
33	Madden, James S. ('	Partner	W	M	Dec, 1872	27	S				Maine	Maine	Scotland	Miner (Qtz.)	yes	yes	yes	
34	Pearsol, Ern A.	Partner	W	M	Aug, 1865	34	S				Nevada	Kentucky	Missouri	Miner (Qtz.)	yes	yes	yes	
35	Boyd, Alexander	Head	W	M	June, 1836	63	S				New Jersey	Ireland	Scotland	Miner Placer	yes	yes	yes	Own
36	McKinley, Jerome	Head	W	M	Mar, 1834	66	M	43			New York	New York	New York	Miner (Qtz.)	yes	yes	yes	

NAME	RELATION	COLOR RACE	SEX	D.O.B. MO,YR	AGE	S,M, W,D	YRS MAR	MOTH # CH.	# CH. Living	BIRTH PLACE THIS PERSON	BIRTH PLACE FATHER	BIRTH PLACE MOTHER	OCCUPATION	READ	WRITE	SPEAK ENGL	OWN RENT
37 Scott, Joseph P.	Partner	W	M	May, 1852	48	S				Iowa	Kentucky	Kentucky	Miner (Qtz.)	yes	yes	yes	
38 Sinn, Tu (or Tee)	Head	C	M	Jan, 1841	59	S				China 1860 Al	China	China	Miner Placer	no	no	yes	Own
39 Healy, Patrick	Head	W	M	Mar, 1802	92	S				Ireland 1815Na	Ireland	Ireland		yes	yes	yes	Rent
40 Patten, Frank K. (?)	Head	W	M	Jan, 1876	24	S				California	Missouri	Maine	Miner (Qtz.)	yes	yes	yes	Own
41 McAtee, Charles	Head	W	M	Sept, 1851	49	S				Ioway (sic)	Virginia	Scotland	Miner Placer	yes	yes	yes	Own
42 Mill, Charles H.	Partner	W	M	June, 1851	48	M	26			England1868Na	England	England	Miner Placer	yes	yes	yes	
43 Thomas, Robert J. ?	Head	W	M	Nov, 1819	80	W				Virginia	Virginia	Virginia		yes	yes	yes	
44 West, Charles H.	Partner	W	M	Aug, 1854	45	W				Tennessee	England	England	Miner (Qtz.)	yes	yes	yes	
45 Thomas, Annie (?)	Head	?	F	Jan, 1866	34	W		4	2	California	Maine	California	Farmer	yes	yes	yes	Own
46 _____ Nancy J.	Daughter	?	F	Feb, 1890	10	S				California	California	California		no	no	yes	
47 Miller, John E.	Boarder	W	M	Aug, 1859	40	S				Pennsylvania	Germany	Germany	Day laborer	yes	yes	yes	
48 Noble, Frank	Boarder	?	M	Dec, 1873	26	S				California	Maine	California	Day laborer	yes	yes	yes	
49 Martin, Robert	Boarder	?	M	Oct, 1871	28	S		1	1	California	Pennsylvania	California	Day laborer	yes	yes	yes	
50 Auck ?, Son ?	Boarder	?	M	Feb, 1833	67	S				China 1856	China	China	Day laborer	no	no	yes	
51 Noble, William	Head	? 1/2	M	May, 1867	33	M	5			California	Maine	California	Miner (Placer)	yes	yes	yes	Own
52 _____ Rosie	Wife	M,I 1/2	F	May, 1878	22	M	5	2	2	California	Ohio	California		yes	yes	yes	
53 _____ William R.	Son	M,I 1/2	M	Mar, 1896	4	S				California	California	California		no	no		
54 _____ Stephen	Son	M,I 1/2	M	Apr, 1899	1	S				California	California	California		no	no		
55 Noble, Stephen	Head	W	M	July, 1832	67	M	35			Maine	Maine	Canada(Scot)	Farmer	yes	yes	yes	Own
56 _____ Sarah	Wife	I	F	Feb, 1855	45	M	35	9	8	California	California	California		no	no	yes	
57 Bowlin ?, John	Boarder	W	M	May, 1829	71	D				England1830Na	England	England	Miner Placer	yes	yes	yes	
58 Patterson, Moses	Head	W	M	Jan, 1822	78	Wd				New York	Vermont	Vermont		yes	yes	yes	Own
59 Scott, Sylvester D.	Boarder	W	M	June, 1829	70	S				Ohio	New York	Ohio	Day laborer	yes	yes	yes	
60 Patterson, James H.	Head	W	M	Sept, 1855	44	M	14			California	New York	Illinois	`Farmer	yes	yes	yes	Own
61 _____ James B.	Son	W	M	Apr, 1883	17	S				California	California	Switzerland	Day laborer	yes	yes	yes	
62 _____ Fred H.	Son	W	M	May, 1884	16	S				California	California	Switzerland	Day laborer	yes	yes	yes	
63 Bonetti, James E.	Boarder	W	M	Oct, 1854	45	M	25			Switzerland	Switzerland	Switzerland	Miner (Placer)	yes	yes	yes	
64 Brown, Sycurger (?)	Head	W	M	Dec, 1871	28	M	6			West Virginia	West Virginia	West Virginia	Miner (Qtz.)	yes	yes	yes	Rent
65 _____ Millie M.	Wife	W	F	Feb, 1869	31	M	6			Indiana	Indiana	Pennsylvania		yes	yes	yes	
66 Dyer, Martha	Head	M,I 1/2	F	June, 1866	33	S				California	Maine	California	Farmer	yes	yes	yes	Own
67 _____ George	Brother	M,I 1/2	M	Oct, 1864	35	S				California	Maine	California	Miner (Placer)	yes	yes	yes	
68 _____ Mary	Mother	I	F	Aug, 1849	50	W				California	California	California		no	no	yes	
69 Bennett, William M.	Boarder	W	M	May, 1860	40	S				New York	Ireland	Ireland	Day laborer	yes	yes	yes	
70 Hackelman, John	Head	W	M	Aug, 1827	72	S				Indiana	So. Carolina	Kentucky	Miner (Placer)	yes	yes	yes	Own
71 Irving, Katie	Head	W	F	Jan, 1864	36	M	16	9	8	Ireland	Scotland	Ireland	Farmer	yes	yes	yes	Own
72 _____ Thomas	Son	W	M	Dec, 1884	15	S				Pennsylvania	Canada	Ireland	Farm laborer	yes	yes	yes	
73 _____ James J.	Son	W	M	Nov, 1886	13	S				Arizona	Canada	Ireland	Farm laborer	yes	yes	yes	
74 _____ George W.	Son	W	M	July, 1889	10	S				California	Canada	Ireland	Farm laborer	yes	yes	yes	
75 _____ Harrison	Son	W	M	Jan, 1891	9	S				California	Canada	Ireland		no	no		
76 _____ Anabella E.	Daughter	W	F	Apr, 1892	8	S				California	Canada	Ireland		no	no		

175

	NAME	RELATION	COLOR RACE	SEX	D.O.B. MO,YR	AGE	S,M, W,D	YRS MAR	MOTH # CH. # CH.	CH. Living	BIRTH PLACE THIS PERSON	BIRTH PLACE FATHER	BIRTH PLACE MOTHER	OCCUPATION	READ	WRITE	SPEAK ENGL	OWN RENT
77	_____ Frank H.	Son	W	M	Apr, 1893	7	S				California	Canada	Ireland		no	no		
78	_____ Leroy	Son	W	M	July, 1895	4	S				California	Canada	Ireland		no	no		
79	_____ Katie M.	Daughter	W	F	May, 1898	2	S				California	Canada	Ireland					
80	Nichols, Mary K. ?	Head	W	F	Dec, 1869	30	M	6	4	4	Wisconsin	Germany	Germany		yes	yes	yes	Own
81	_____ Catherine D.	Daughter	W	F	June 1894	5	S				California	Wisconsin	Wisconsin		no	no		
82	_____ Nelson E.	Son	W	M	Feb, 1895	4	S				California	Wisconsin	Wisconsin		no	no		
83	_____ William I. ?	Son	W	M	Feb, 1896	4	S				California	Wisconsin	Wisconsin		no	no		
84	_____ Charles B.	Son	W	M	Oct, 1898	1	S				California	Wisconsin	Wisconsin					
85	Smith, Jessie	Head	W	M	Apr, 1836	64	S				Pennsylvania	Pennsylvania	Pennsylvania	Farmer	yes	yes	yes	Own
86	Corning, Stephen	Boarder	W	M	Nov, 1876	23	S				California	New York	New York	Farm Laborer	yes	yes	yes	
87	Martin, William	Boarder	M,I 1/2	M	Feb, 1879	21	S				California	Pennsylvania	California	Farm laborer	yes	yes	yes	
88	Ach, Ah	Head	CL?	M	Jan, 1851	49	S				China 1869 Al	China	China	Miner (Placer)	yes	yes	yes	Own
89	Chong, Ah	Head	CL?	M	Mar, 1861	39	S				China 1881 Al	China	China	Miner (Placer)	no	no	yes	Own
90	Corning, Smith P.	Head	W	M	Oct, 1830	69	Wd				New York	Ohio	Maine	Miner (Placer)	yes	yes	yes	Own
91	Zeigler, Jeanette ?	Head	W	F	Apr, 1856	43	D		3	3	California	Maine	California	Farmer	yes	yes	yes	Own
92	_____ Bjorn (?) W.	Son	W	M	Sept, 1878	21	M	4			California	Ohio	California	Farm Laborer	yes	yes	yes	
93	_____ Charles B.	Son	W	M	July, 1880	19	S				California	Ohio	California	Farm laborer	yes	yes	yes	
94	_____ Hiram W.	Son	W	M	Nov, 1886	13	S				California	Ohio	California	At School	yes	yes	yes	
95	_____ Mable R.	D-in-law ?	W	F	Dec, 1880	19	M	4	3	3	California	New York	New York		yes	yes	yes	
96	_____ Seri (?) E.	Grandson	W	M	Mar, 1897	3	S				California	California	California		no	no		
97	_____ Cora W.	Daughter	W	F	Mar, 1898	2	S				California	California	California		no	no		
98	_____ Adelle J.	Daughter	W	F	Feb, 1900	3 mo					California	California	California					
99	Howell?, Charles	Head	W	M	Mar, 1848	52	M	5			Maine	England	Maine	Farmer	yes	yes	yes	Own
100	_____?, Emilie ?	Wife	W	F	Dec, 1870	29	M	5			California	Maine	California		?	?	?	
101	_____? Julia	Daughter	W	F	Dec, 1895	4	S				California	Maine	California		no	no		
102	_____? Fred	Son	W	M	Aug, 1897	2	S				California	Maine	California					
103	Schaber, John	Head	W	M	Dec, 1851	48	S				German1845Na	Germany	Germany	Miner (Placer)	yes	yes	yes	?
104	Campbell, Mary	Head	I	F	Swx, 1851	48	Wd		10	7	California	California	California	Farmer	no	no	yes	?
105	_____ James	Son	M,I 1/2	M	Nov, 1881	18	S				California	Missouri	California	Farm laborer	yes	yes	yes	?
106	Dart, Jessie	Daughter	M,I 1/2	F	June, 1879	20	M	3	0	0	California	Missouri	California		yes	yes	yes	?
107	Ferguson, Martha	Daughter	M,I 1/2	F	Jan, 1872	28	M	1	0	0	California	Missouri	California		yes	yes	yes	?
108	Kinsey, Ronnie	Grandson	M,I 1/4	M	Nov, 1891	8	S				California	Ohio	California	At school				
109	Ferguson, Charles	S-in-law	W	M	Aug,. 1872	27	M	1			Indiana	Indiana	Indiana	Farm Laborer	yes	yes	yes	?
110	Campbell, William	Head	M,I 1/2	M	Jan, 1870	30	M	3			California	Missouri	California	Packer (trains)	yes	yes	yes	?
111	_____ Mary V.	Wife	M,I 1/4	F	Nov, 1878	21	M	3	2	1	California	Illinois	California		yes	yes	yes	
112	_____ Hyacinth I.?	Daughter	M,I 1/4	F	Mar, 1898	2	S				California	California	California					
113	Walker, Sizzie/Siggle	S-in-law ?	M,I 1/4	F	Mar, 1887	13	S				California	Illinois	California	At school	yes	yes	yes	
114	Ferguson, Thomas J	Boarder	W	M	Jan, 1850	50	Wd				Indiana	Indiana	Indiana	Day laborer	yes	yes	yes	?
115	Timley?, Agustus	Head	W	M	Mar, 1878	22	M	0			California	Virginia	Ohio	Farmer	yes	yes	yes	Own
116	_____? Eliza J.	Wife	M,I 1/2	F	Aug, 1873	26	M	0	1	1	California	Kentucky	California		yes	yes	yes	

176

NAME	RELATION	COLOR RACE	SEX	D.O.B. MO,YR	AGE	S,M, W,D	YRS MAR	MOTH # CH.	# CH. Living	BIRTH PLACE THIS PERSON	BIRTH PLACE FATHER	BIRTH PLACE MOTHER	OCCUPATION	READ	WRIT	SPEAK ENGL	OWN/ RENT
117 _____? Gladys M.	Daughter	M,I 1/4	F	May, 1900	1 mc	S				California	California	California					
118 Donahue, John W.	Head	W	M	Jan, 1862	37	M	14			Michigan	Ireland	Ireland	Farmer	yes	yes	yes	Own
119 _____ Ida	Wife	W	F	Ixrm 1864	35	M	14	2	2	Michigan	Ohio	Kentucky		yes	yes	yes	
120 _____ Jay S.	Son	W	M	Mar, 1888	12	S				Michigan	Michigan	Michigan	At school	yes	yes	yes	
121 _____ Ethel E.	Daughter	W	F	Nov, 1890	9	S				Michigan	Michigan	Michigan	At school	yes	yes	yes	
122 Hammer, Peter P.	Head	W	M	June, 1847	52	D				Germany1849N	Germany	Germany	Miner placer	yes	yes	yes	Own
123 Kahlke, Jacob	Partner	W	M	Mar, 1852	48	S				Germany1870N	Germany	Germany	Miner placer	yes	yes	yes	
124 Konn, John A.	Head	W	M	July, 1844	55	M	13			New York	Germany	Germany	Farmer	yes	yes	yes	Own
125 _____ Cora ?	Wife	M,I 1/2	F	Feb, 1865	35	M	13	7	7	California	California	California		yes	yes	yes	
126 _____ Ida	Daughter	M,I 1/4	F	Mar, 1886	14	S				California	New York	California	At School	yes	yes	yes	
127 _____ Caroline	Daughter	M,I 1/4	F	Sept, 1887	12	S				California	New York	California	At School	yes	yes	yes	
128 _____ Arthur A.	Son	M,I 1/4	M	Oct, 1888	11	S				California	New York	California	At School	yes	yes	yes	
129 _____ Gorggie ? S.	Son	M,I 1/4	M	Dec, 1890	9	S				California	New York	California	At School	yes	yes		
130 _____ Roswell	Son	M,I 1/4	M	July, 1892	7	S				California	New York	California	At School				
131 _____ Cora E.	Daughter	M,I 1/4	F	Mar, 1894	6	S				California	New York	California	At School				
132 Berg, Anton	Head	W	M	Aug, 1862	37	A				Minnesota	Minnesota	Sweden	Miner (placer)	yes	yes	yes	Own
133 Try?, Louis	Head	W	M	Swxc, 1838	61	S				Switzer1869Pa	Switzerland	Switzerland	Miner (placer)	yes	yes	yes	Own
134 Swanson, O, A	Head	W	M	Dec, 1854	45	S				Sweden1880Na	Sweden	Sweden	Miner (placer)	yes	yes	yes	Own
135 Gray, David B.	Head	W	M	Aug, 1832	67	M	28			Pennsylvania	Pennsylvania	Germany	Miner (placer)	yes	yes	yes	Own
136 _____ Minnie A.	Wife	W	F	Jan, 1844	56	M	28	3	3	Pennsylvania	Pennsylvania	Pennsylvania		yes	yes	yes	
137 _____ William H.	Son	W	M	July, 1873	26	S				California	Pennsylvania	Pennsylvania	Day laborer	yes	yes	yes	
138 _____ David H. M.	Son	W	M	Aug, 1876	23	S				California	Pennsylvania	Pennsylvania	Day laborer	yes	yes	yes	
139 _____ Blanche	Daughter	W	F	May, 1880	20	S				California	Pennsylvania	Pennsylvania		yes	yes	yes	
140 Gee, Ah	Head	CL?	M	Feb, 1835	65	S				China1860 Al	China	China	Miner (placer)	no	no	yes	Rent
141 Smith, Gamaliff ?	Head	W	M	Feb, 1854	46	S				Canada (Eng)	Canada (Eng)	Canada (Eng.)	Miner (placer)	yes	yes	yes	Own
142 Warrington, William	Partner	W	M	Sept, 1856	43	S				England1879Na	England	England	Miner (placer)	yes	yes	yes	
143 Barber, John W. M.	Head	W	M	Sept, 1854	45	S				Pennsylvania	Pennsylvania	Pennsylvania	Miner (placer)	yes	yes	yes	Own
144 Hennessey, Patrick	Head	W	M	Feb, 1829	71	M	37			Ireland1850Na	Ireland	Ireland	Farmer	yes	yes	yes	Own
145 _____ Marie	Wife	W	F	Jan, 1847	53	M	37	9	7	Ireland (Un)	Ireland	Ireland		yes	yes	yes	
146 _____ Esther	Daughter	W	F	June, 1868	31	S				California	Ireland	Ireland		yes	yes	yes	
147 _____ Richard W.	Son	W	M	May, 1879	20	S				California	Ireland	Ireland	Farm laborer	yes	yes	yes	
148 _____ Katie	Daughter	W	F	May, 1879	20	S				California	Ireland	Ireland		yes	yes	yes	
149 Keeley, Margaret	M-in-law	W	F	Noc, 1822	77	M		1	1	Ireland (Un)	Ireland	Ireland		yes	yes	yes	
150 Sintozi?, Roswell	Head	W	M	Nov, 1847?	52?	S				Maine	Maine	Maine	Carpenter	yes	yes	yes	Own
151 McWharton, Adison?	Head	W	M	Apr, 1824	76	M	31			New York	New York	New York	Farmer	yes	yes	yes	Own
152 _____ Barbara	Wife	W	F	Sept, 1829	70	M	31	1	1	Germany (Un)	Germany	Germany		yes	yes	yes	
153 McDonald, Pauline	Daughter	W	F	June, 1870	29	N	12	4	4	California	New York	Germany		yes	yes	yes	
154 _____ James D.	Son-in-law	W	M	Nov, 1858	41	M	12			California	Missouri	Indiana	Mail contracto	yes	yes	yes	
155 _____ Ethel W.	G.Daughte	W	F	Dec, 1887	12	S				California	California	California	At School	yes	yes	yes	
156 _____ Idell B.	G.Daughte	W	F	Nov, 1890	9	S				California	California	California	At School	yes	yes	yes	

NAME	RELATION	COLOR RACE	SEX	D.O.B. MO,YR	AGE	S,M, W,D	YRS MAR	MOTH # CH.	# CH. Living	BIRTH PLACE THIS PERSON	BIRTH PLACE FATHER	BIRTH PLACE MOTHER	OCCUPATION	READ	WRITE	SPEAK ENGL	OWN/ RENT
157 _____ Albert W.	G.son	W	M	Dec, 1892	7	S					California	California	California	At School				
158 _____ Hilton V. B.	G.son	W	M	Jan, 1895	5	S					California	California	California	At School				
159 Sharon?, James M.	Boarder	W	M	May, 1831	79(?	S					Kentucky	Kentucky	Kentucky		yes	yes	yes	
160 Koons, Arthur	Boarder	W	M	Oct, 1888	11	S					California	New York	New York	At School	yes	yes	yes	
161 Wildes?, Corinne	Boarder	W	F	May, 1880	20	S					Nevada	Maine	Indiana	Teacher(schoo	yes	yes	yes	
162 Thurban?, Albert	Head	W	M	Sept, 1828	71	Wd					Rhode Island	Rhode Island	Rhode Island	Day laborer	yes	yes	yes	tent
163 Frank, Gus ?	Partner	W	M	Dec, 1876	223	S					So. Dakota	Germany	Germany	Day laborer	yes	yes	yes	
164 Moody, William	Head	W	M	Dec, 1862	37	M	11				Illinois	Kentucky	Missouri	Miner (placer)	yes	yes	yes	Own
165 _____ Catherine D.	Wife	W	F	May, 1864	36	M	11	0	0	Scotland	Scotland	Scotland		yes	yes	yes	
166 Thurber, Clinton	Head	W	M	Apr, 1863	37	S					California	Rhode Island	Massachusetts	Day laborer	yes	yes	yes	tent

INDIAN POPULATION

NAME	RELATION	COLOR RACE	SEX	D.O.B. MO,YR	AGE	S,M, W,D	YRS MAR	MOTH # CH.	# CH. Living	BIRTH PLACE THIS PERSON	BIRTH PLACE FATHER	BIRTH PLACE MOTHER	OCCUPATION	READ	WRITE	SPEAK ENGL	OWN/ RENT
167 Chesbrow, James	Head	I. 1/2	M	Sept, 1857	42	M	2			California	California	California	Mail carrier	yes	no	yes	Rent
168 _____ Ellen	Wife	I. 1/2	F	Feb, 1883	17	M	2	2	1	California	California	California		no	no	yes	
169 _____ Mary	Daughter	I. 1/2	F	Jan, 1900	4 mo	S				California	California	California					
170 Noble, Georgia	Boarder	I. 1/2	F	Aug, 1886	13	S				California	California	California	At school	yes	yes	yes	
171 Noble, Fredrick	Boarder	I. 1/2	M	May, 1888	12	S				California	California	California	At school	yes	yes	yes	
172 Johnnie Indian	Head	I	M	Nov, 1853	46	M	24			California	California	California	Day laborer	no	no	yes	Own
173 _____ Nellie	Wife	I	F	Awpt, 1859	49	M	24	4	1	California	California	California		no	no	yes	
174 _____ Minnie	Daughter	I	F	Feb, 1893	7	S				California	California	California					

SPECIAL INQUIRIES RELATING TO INDIANS

NAME	TRIBE	TRIBE- FATHER	TRIBE- MOTHER	ANY WHITE BLOOD?	LIVING IN POLYGAMY?	TAXED?	YR. CITIZEN?	CITIZENSHIP BY ALLOTMENT?	LIVING IN FIXED OR MOVABLE DWELLING?
167 Chesbrow, James	Hoopa Valley	Hoopa Valley	Hoopa Valley	Half	No	Yes	1888	No	Fixed
168 _____ Ellen	Hoopa Valley	Hoopa Valley	Hoopa Valley	0	No				
169 _____ Mary	Hoopa Valley	Hoopa Valley	Hoopa Valley	Half					
170 Noble, Georgia			Klamath	Half					
171 Noble, Fredrick			Klamath	Half					
172 Johnnie Indian	Hoopa Valley	Hoopa Valley	Hoopa Valley	0	No	Yes		No	Fixed
173 _____ Nellie	Hoopa Valley	Hoopa Valley	Hoopa Valley	0	No				
174 _____ Minnie	Hoopa Valley	Hoopa Valley	Hoopa Valley	0					

INDEX

183